Leckie × Leckie
Scotland's leading educational publishers

D1080761

MORE

Practice Papers for SQA Exams

Higher

Mathematics

Introduction	3
Practice Exam D	7
Practice Exam E	23
Practice Exam F	39
Answers	53

NOTE

Practice Exams A, B, C
and their answers are in
ISBN: 978-1-84372-783-5
Practice Papers for SQA Exams—
Higher Mathematics

01/040311

ISBN: 978-1-84372-873-3

Published by
Leckie & Leckie Ltd
An imprint of HarperCollins*Publishers*
Westerhill Road, Bishopbriggs, Glasgow G64 2QT
T: 0844 576 8126 F: 0844 576 8131
leckieandleckie@harpercollins.co.uk www.leckieandleckie.co.uk

Special thanks to
Exemplarr (layout and illustration),
Caleb O' Loan (proofread), Tara Watson (proofread)
Peter Crampton (proofread), Helen Bleck (proofread)

A CIP Catalogue record for this book is available from the British Library.

Questions and answers in this book do not emanate from SQA. All of our entirely new and original Practice Papers have been written by experienced authors working directly for the publisher.

Introduction

More Practice!

This book contains brand new practice exams, which mirror the actual SQA exam as closely as possible in question style, level, layout and paper colour. It is a perfect way to familiarise yourself with what the exam papers you will sit will look like.

The answer section at the back of the book contains fully worked answers to each question, letting you know exactly where marks are gained in an answer and how the right answer is arrived at. It is also packed with explanatory notes, helpful advice and hints to maximise your understanding of the types of questions you're likely to face in the exam. The answers also include helpful cross-references to Leckie & Leckie's book: "Higher Maths Revision Notes" (HMRN).

As the name suggests, this book is a volume of More Practice Exam Papers for Higher Mathematics. Its sister publication (ISBN: 978-1-84372-783-5 Higher Mathematics Practice Papers for SQA Exams) is also available and packed full of entirely different practice exams, worked solutions and helpful explanations, hints and exam tips.

How To Use This Book

The Practice Papers can be used in two main ways:

1. You can complete an entire practice paper as preparation for the final exam. If you would like to use the book in this way, you can either complete the practice paper under exam-style conditions by setting yourself a time for each paper and answering it as well as possible without using any references or notes. Alternatively, you can answer the practice paper questions as a revision exercise, using your notes to produce a model answer. Your teacher may mark these for you.
2. You can use the Topic Index at the front of this book to find all the questions within the book that deal with a specific topic. This allows you to focus specifically on areas that you particularly want to revise or if you are mid-way through your course, it lets you practise answering exam-style questions for just those topics that you have studied.

Revision Advice

Work out a revision timetable for each week's work in advance – remember to cover all of your subjects and to leave time for homework and breaks. For example:

Day	6pm–6.45pm	7pm–8pm	8.15pm–9pm	9.15pm–10pm
Monday	Homework	Homework	English Revision	Chemistry Revision
Tuesday	Maths Revision	Physics Revision	Homework	Free
Wednesday	Geography Revision	Modern Studies Revision	English Revision	French Revision
Thursday	Homework	Maths Revision	Chemistry Revision	Free
Friday	Geography Revision	French Revision	Free	Free
Saturday	Free	Free	Free	Free
Sunday	Modern Studies Revision	Maths Revision	Modern Studies Revision	Homework

Make sure that you have at least one evening free a week to relax, socialise and re-charge your batteries. It also gives your brain a chance to process the information that you have been feeding it all week.

Arrange your study time into one hour or 30 minute sessions, with a break between sessions, e.g. 6pm–7pm, 7.15pm–7.45pm, 8pm–9pm. Try to start studying as early as possible in the evening when your brain is still alert and be aware that the longer you put off starting, the harder it will be to start!

Study a different subject in each session, except for the day before an exam.

Do something different during your breaks between study sessions – have a cup of tea, or listen to some music. Don't let your 15 minutes expand into 20 or 25 minutes though!

Have your class notes and any textbooks available for your revision to hand as well as plenty of blank paper, a pen, etc. You should take note of any topic area that you are having particular difficulty with, as and when the difficulty arises. Revisit that question later having revised that topic area by attempting some further questions from the exercises in your textbook.

Revising for a Maths Exam is different from revising for some of your other subjects. Revision is only effective if you are trying to solve problems. You may like to make a list of 'Key Questions' with the dates of your various attempts (successful or not!). These should be questions that you have had real difficulty with.

Key Question	1st Attempt		2nd Attempt		3rd Attempt	
Textbook P56 Q3a	18/2/11	X	21/2/11	✓	28/2/11	✓
Practice Exam D Paper1 Q5	25/2/11	X	28/2/11	X	3/3/11	
2008 SQA Paper, Paper2 Q4c	27/2/11	X	2/3/11			

The method for working this list is as follows:

1. Any attempt at a question should be dated.
2. A tick or cross should be entered to mark the success or failure of each attempt.
3. A date for your next attempt at that question should be entered:

   for an unsuccessful attempt – 3 days later

   for a successful attempt – 1 week later
4. After two successful attempts remove that question from the list (you can assume the question has been learnt!)

Using 'The List' method for revising for your Maths exam ensures that your revision is focused on the difficulties you have had and that you are actively trying to overcome these difficulties.

Finally, forget or ignore all or some of the advice in this section if you are happy with your present way of studying. Everyone revises differently, so find a way that works for you!

Transfer Your Knowledge

As well as using your class notes and textbooks to revise, these practice papers will also be a useful revision tool as they will help you to get used to answering exam-style questions. You may find as you work through the questions that you come across an example that you haven't seen before. Don't worry! There may be several reasons for this. You may have come across a question on a topic that you have not yet covered in class. Check with your teacher to find out. Or it may be that the wording or the context of the question is unfamiliar. This often happens with reasoning questions in the Maths exam. Once you have familiarised yourself with the worked solutions you will find that, in most cases, the question is using mathematical techniques which you are familiar with. In either case you should revisit that question later to check that you can successfully solve it.

Trigger Words

In the practice papers and in the exam itself, a number of 'trigger words' will be used in the questions. These trigger words should help you identify a process or a technique that is expected in your solution to that part of the question. If you familiarise yourself with these trigger words, it will help you to structure your solutions more effectively.

Trigger Word	Meaning / Explanation
Evaluate	Carry out a calculation to give an answer that is a value.
Hence	You must use the result of the previous part of the question to complete your solution. No marks will be given if you use an alternative method that does not use the previous answer.

Simplify	This means different things in different contexts: Surds: reduce the number under the root sign to the smallest possible by removing square factors. Fractions: one fraction, cancelled down, is expected. Algebraic expressions: get rid of brackets and gather all like terms together.
Give your answer to...	This is an instruction for the accuracy of your final answer. These instructions must be followed or you will lose a mark.
Algebraically	The method you use must involve algebra, e.g. you must solve an equation or simplify an algebraic expression. It is usually stated to avoid trial-and-improvement methods or reading answers from your calculator.
Justify your answer	This is a request for you to clearly indicate your reasoning. Will the examiner know how your answer was obtained?
Show all your working	Marks will be allocated for the individual steps in your working. Steps missed out may lose you marks.

In the Exam

Watch your time and pace yourself carefully. You will find some questions harder than others. Try not to get stuck on one question as you may run out of time later. Rather, return to a difficult question later. Remember also that if you have spare time towards the end of your exam, use it to check through your solutions. Mistakes are often discovered in this checking process and can be corrected.

Become familiar with the exam instructions. The practice papers in this book have the exam instructions at the front of each exam. Also remember that there is a formulae list to consult. You will find this at the front of your exam paper. However, even though these formulae are given to you, it is important that you learn them so that they are familiar to you. If you are continuing with Mathematics it will be assumed that these formulae are known in next year's exam!

Read the question thoroughly before you begin to answer it – make sure you know exactly what the question is asking you to do. If the question is in sections, e.g. 15a, 15b, 15c, etc, then it is often the case that answers obtained in the earlier sections are used in the later sections of that question.

When you have completed your solution read it over again. Is your reasoning clear? Will the examiner understand how you arrived at your answer? If in doubt then fill in more details.

If you change your mind or think that your solution is wrong, don't score it out unless you have another solution to replace it with. Solutions that are not correct can often gain some of the marks available. Do not miss working out. Showing step-by-step working will help you gain maximum marks even if there is a mistake in the working.

Use these resources constructively by reworking questions later that you found difficult or impossible first time round. Remember: success in a Maths exam will only come from actively trying to solve lots of questions and only consulting notes when you are stuck. Reading notes alone is not a good way to revise for your Maths exam. Always be active, always solve problems.

Good luck!

Topic Index

Topic	D Paper 1	D Paper 2	E Paper 1	E Paper 2	F Paper 1	F Paper 2	Knowledge for Prelim			Knowledge for SQA Exam		
							Have difficulty	Still needs work	Ok	Have difficulty	Still needs work	Ok
Unit 1												
• The Straight Line	1, 22, 23		3, 4, 14, 22		2, 4, 21							
• Functions and Graphs	2, 9, 20		9, 24	3	1, 8							
• Trig – Basic Facts	7		12			8						
• Intro to Differentiation	13, 14, 15, 21	5	5, 6, 19	2		5						
• Recurrence Relations	3, 6		2, 7		7, 22							
Unit 2												
• Polynomials	17, 21			1	25	9						
• Quadratic Theory	4, 11, 19		13, 20		6, 26	9						
• Intro to Integration	16	7	17			2, 6						
• Further Trig	23	3	8, 10, 23	4	10, 11, 17, 19	1, 8						
• Circles	10	6	1, 11	5	3, 9, 26	4						
Unit 3												
• Vectors	5, 12	2	18, 21	8	16, 18, 23	3						
• Further Diff & Int	8	4, 7	16	4	5, 12, 13							
• Log & Exp Functions	18	8		6, 7	14, 15, 20	7						
• Wave Function		1	15		24							

Practice Exam D

Mathematics Higher

Practice Papers
For SQA Exams

Exam D
Higher
Paper 1
Non-calculator

You are allowed 1 hour, 30 minutes to complete this paper.

You must **not** use a calculator.

Full marks will only be awarded where your answers include relevant working.

You will not receive any marks for answers derived from scale drawings.

Leckie × Leckie
Scotland's leading educational publishers

FORMULAE LIST

Trigonometric formulae

$$\sin(A \pm B) = \sin A \cos B \pm \cos A \sin B$$
$$\cos(A \pm B) = \cos A \cos B \mp \sin A \sin B$$
$$\sin 2A = 2\sin A \cos A$$
$$\cos 2A = \cos^2 A - \sin^2 A$$
$$= 2\cos^2 A - 1$$
$$= 1 - 2\sin^2 A$$

Circle

The equation $x^2 + y^2 + 2gx + 2fy + c = 0$ represents a circle with centre $(-g, -f)$ and radius $\sqrt{g^2 + f^2 - c}$.

The equation $(x - a)^2 + (y - b)^2 = r^2$ represents a circle with centre (a, b) and radius r.

Table of standard integrals

$f(x)$	$\int f(x)\,dx$
$\sin ax$	$-\frac{1}{a}\cos ax + C$
$\cos ax$	$\frac{1}{a}\sin ax + C$

Table of standard derivatives

$f(x)$	$f'(x)$
$\sin ax$	$a \cos ax$
$\cos ax$	$-a \sin ax$

Scalar Product $\boldsymbol{a} \cdot \boldsymbol{b} = |\boldsymbol{a}||\boldsymbol{b}| \cos\theta$, where θ is the angle between $\boldsymbol{a}$ and $\boldsymbol{b}$

or $\boldsymbol{a} \cdot \boldsymbol{b} = a_1b_1 + a_2b_2 + a_3b_3$ where $\boldsymbol{a} = \begin{pmatrix} a_1 \\ a_2 \\ a_3 \end{pmatrix}$ and $\boldsymbol{b} = \begin{pmatrix} b_1 \\ b_2 \\ b_3 \end{pmatrix}$.

SECTION A

1. The line with equation $y = mx + c$ is parallel to the line with equation $3x + 2y - 1 = 0$. What is the value of m?

A -3

B $-\frac{3}{2}$

C $\frac{1}{2}$

D $\frac{2}{3}$

2. When $2x^2 - 4x + 1$ is written in the form $2(x + a)^2 + b$, what is the value of b?

A -1

B $-\frac{1}{2}$

C 0

D 1

3. A sequence is defined by the recurrence relation $u_{n+1} = -0{\cdot}2u_n + 5$, with $u_0 = 8$.

What is the limit of this sequence?

A $\frac{1}{20}$

B $\frac{25}{6}$

C $\frac{25}{4}$

D 25

4. The roots of the equation $3x^2 - x + c = 0$ are equal. What is the value of c?

A -12

B $-\frac{1}{12}$

C $\frac{1}{12}$

D 12

5. Given that $2\boldsymbol{a} - 3\boldsymbol{b} = \begin{pmatrix} -8 \\ -1 \\ 3 \end{pmatrix}$, where $\boldsymbol{b} = \begin{pmatrix} 2 \\ 1 \\ 5 \end{pmatrix}$, find $\boldsymbol{a}$ in component form.

A $\begin{pmatrix} -1 \\ 1 \\ 9 \end{pmatrix}$

B $\begin{pmatrix} -1 \\ -4 \\ -12 \end{pmatrix}$

C $\begin{pmatrix} -22 \\ -5 \\ -9 \end{pmatrix}$

D $\begin{pmatrix} -22 \\ 1 \\ 21 \end{pmatrix}$

6. A sequence is defined by the recurrence relation

$u_{n+1} = 3u_n - 1$ and $u_0 = \frac{1}{3}$

what is the value of u_2?

A $-\frac{5}{3}$

B -1

C 0

D $\frac{4}{9}$

7. The diagram shows the graph with equation $y = 2\sin ax + b$ where a and b are constants and $0 \leq x \leq \pi$.

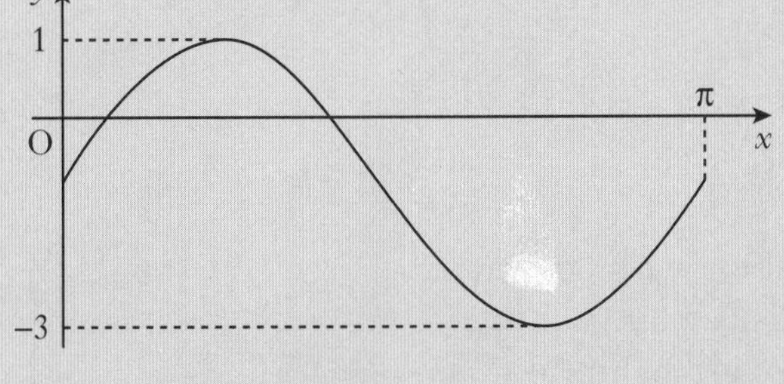

What are the values of a and b?

A $a = \frac{1}{2}, b = -3$

B $a = \frac{1}{2}, b = 1$

C $a = 2, b = -1$

D $a = 4, b = -3$

8. Find $\int (\sin 2x + 2x^{-2})\,dx$.

A $-\frac{1}{2}\cos 2x - 2x^{-1} + C$

B $2\cos 2x - 2x^{-1} + C$

C $\frac{1}{2}\cos 2x + x^{-1} + C$

D $\frac{1}{2}\cos 2x - 4x^{-3} + C$

9. $g(x) = 3x$ and $h(x) = \sin 2x$ are two functions defined on suitable domains.

What is the value of $h\left(g\left(\frac{\pi}{12}\right)\right)$?

A 0

B 1

C $\frac{3}{2}$

D $\sqrt{2}$

10.

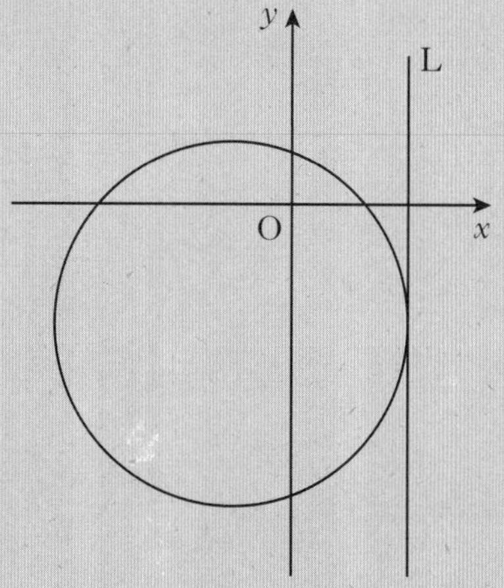

The diagram shows the circle with equation $x^2 + y^2 + 2x + 4y - 4 = 0$.

Line L is a tangent to the circle parallel to the y-axis.

What is the equation of L?

A $x = 1$

B $x = \sqrt{5} - 1$

C $x = 2$

D $x = \sqrt{5}$

11. The diagram shows a parabola with equation $y = ax^2 + bx + c$. The x-axis is a tangent to the parabola. What is the relationship between a, b and c?

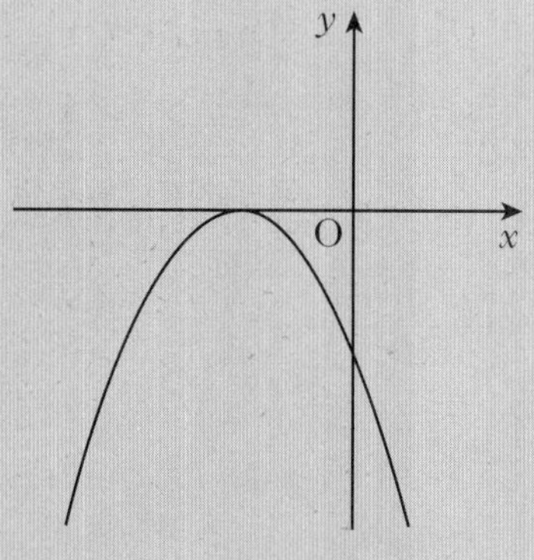

A $b^2 > 4ac$

B $b^2 < 4ac$

C $b^2 = -4ac$

D $b^2 = 4ac$

12. The vectors $\begin{pmatrix} -1 \\ k \\ 3 \end{pmatrix}$ and $\begin{pmatrix} -4 \\ 2 \\ -1 \end{pmatrix}$ are perpendicular. What is the value of k?

A 2

B $\frac{2}{7}$

C 0

D $-\frac{1}{2}$

13. What is the derivative, with respect to x, of $\dfrac{1}{2\sqrt[3]{x}}$?

A $-\frac{1}{6}x^{-\frac{4}{3}}$

B $-\frac{1}{6}x^{\frac{2}{3}}$

C $-3x^{-\frac{5}{2}}$

D $-\frac{2}{3}x^{-\frac{4}{3}}$

14. Which of the following could represent a function f such that $f'(-1)=0$ and $f(1) < 0$?

A

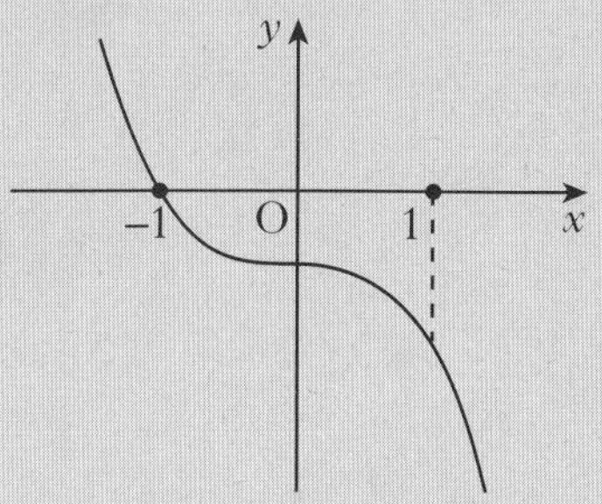

B

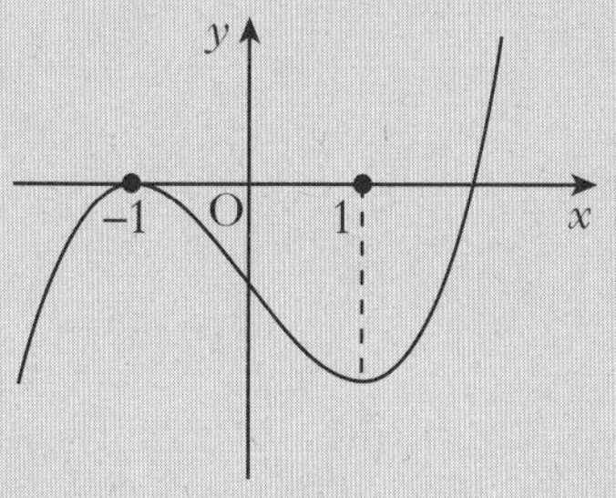

C

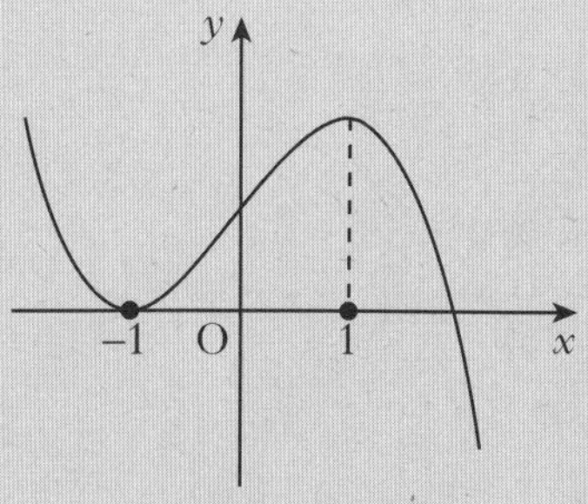

D

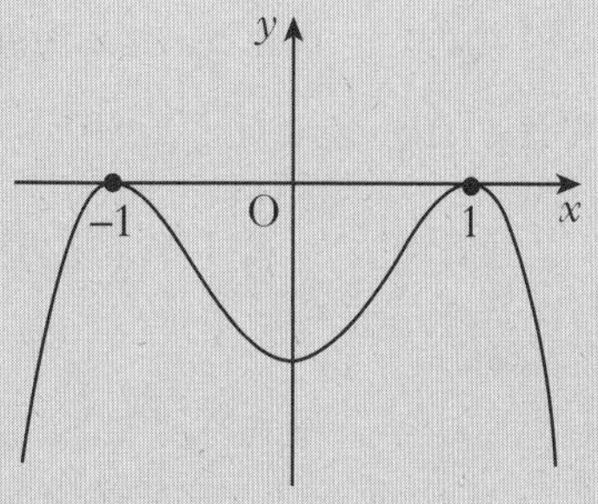

15. If $V(r) = \frac{4}{3}\pi r^3$, what is the rate of change of V with respect to r when $r = 1$?

A 4

B 4π

C 16

D 8π

16. The diagram shows the graphs of functions f and g. Here are two statements concerning the diagram:

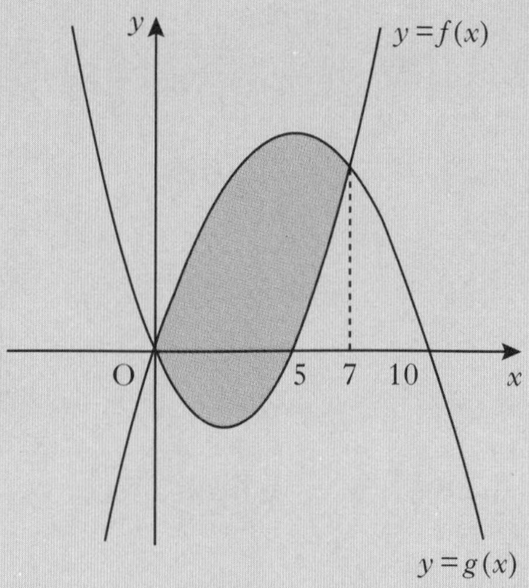

(1) The shaded area is given by

$$\int_0^7 g(x)\,dx - \int_0^5 f(x)\,dx$$

(2) The shaded area is given by

$$\int_0^{10} g(x)\,dx - \int_5^{10} f(x)\,dx - \int_0^5 f(x)\,dx$$

Which of the following is true?

A Neither statement is correct.

B Only statement (1) is correct.

C Only statement (2) is correct.

D Both statements are correct.

17. The diagram shows part of the graph of a cubic function with equation

$y = m(x + n)(x + 1)(x + 2)$.

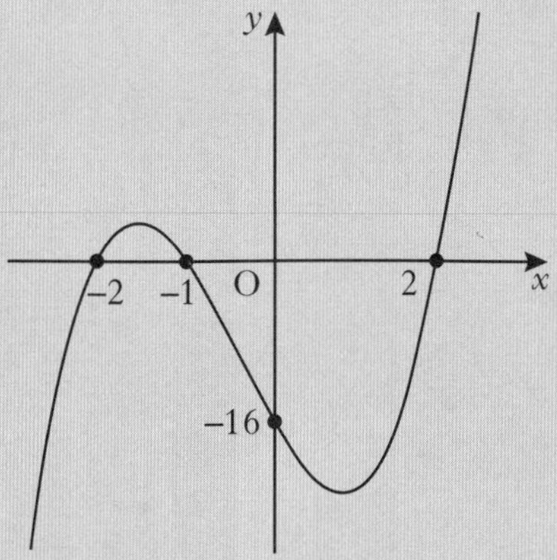

What are the values of m and n?

	m	n
A	–4	–2
B	–4	2
C	4	–2
D	4	2

18. The diagram shows a graph with equation of the form $y = \log_b(x + a)$ where a and b are constants.

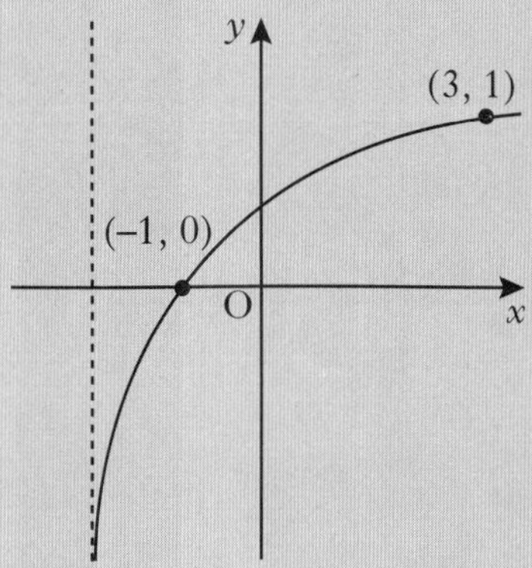

What is the equation of the graph?

A $y = \log_3(x - 2)$

B $y = \log_3(x + 2)$

C $y = \log_5(x - 2)$

D $y = \log_5(x + 2)$

19. A function f is defined on the set of Real numbers by $f(x) = 2x^2 + 5x - 3$.

Find the solution of $f(x) < 0$.

A $-3 < x < \frac{1}{2}$

B $-\frac{1}{2} < x < 3$

C $x < -3,\ x > \frac{1}{2}$

D $x < -\frac{1}{2},\ x > 3$

20. The graph $y = 3f\left(\frac{1}{2}x\right)$ has a minimum stationary point at (–6, 12).

Find the coordinates of the corresponding minimum stationary point on the graph $y = f(x)$.

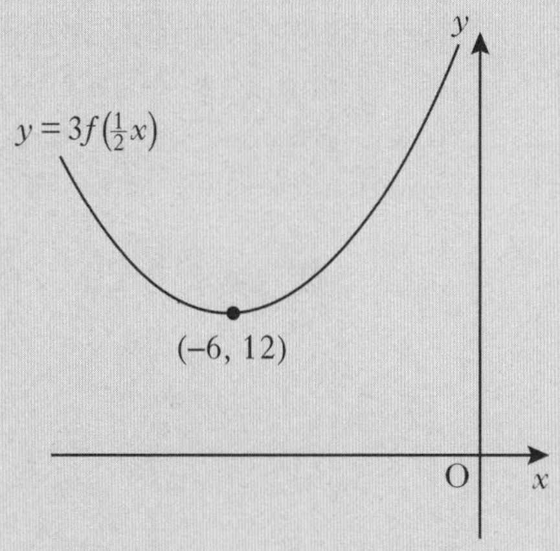

A (–12, 4)

B (–3, 4)

C (–2, 6)

D (–2, 36)

[End of section A]

SECTION B

Marks

21. The functions f, g and h are defined on the set of Real numbers by:

$f(x) = 2x^3 + x - 3$

$g(x) = -3x^2 + x - 2$

$h(x) = 2x^3 + 3x^2 - 1$

(*a*) (i) Show that $x + 1$ is a factor of $h(x)$.

(ii) Hence factorise $h(x)$ fully.

(iii) Solve $h(x) = 0$. **5**

(*b*) The two curves $y = f(x)$ and $y = g(x)$ share a common tangent at point T. Find the coordinates of T. **6**

22.

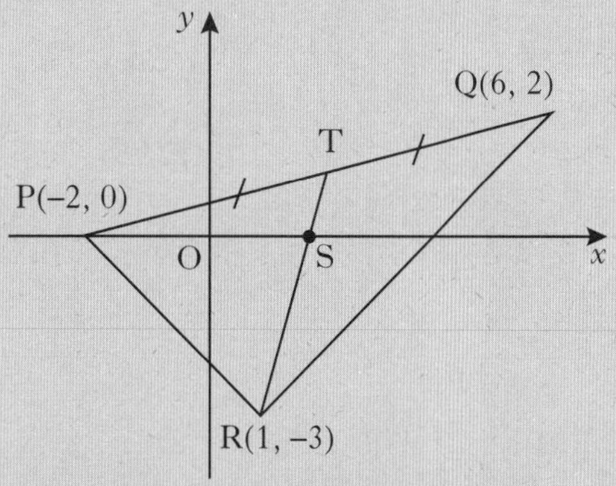

Triangle PQR has vertices P(−2, 0), Q(6, 2) and R(1, −3). The median RT crosses the x-axis at the point S as shown in the diagram.

(*a*) Find the equation of RT. **3**

(*b*) Find the coordinates of the point S. **1**

(*c*) Find the ratio in which S divides RT. **2**

23. Line L has equation $3y - x = 0$. Triangle OAB is right-angled at point A, which lies on the x-axis. Point B lies on line L. Triangle OBC is right-angled at B, with point C lying on line M. OB and BC are equal in length.

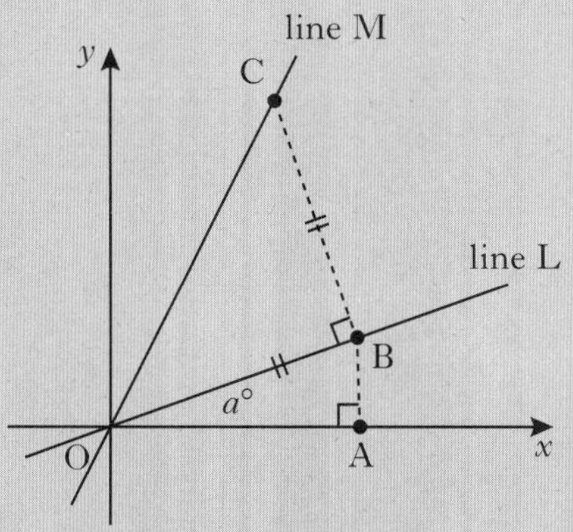

(*a*) Show that $\tan a° = \frac{1}{3}$. **2**

(*b*) Hence find the exact value of $\sin a°$. **2**

(*c*) Show that $\sin(a + 45)° = \frac{2\sqrt{5}}{5}$. **5**

(*d*) If OC = 5 units, use the result in (*c*) above to calculate the exact value of the y-coordinate of the point C. **2**

(*e*) Find the equation of line M. **2**

[End of section B]

[End of question paper]

Mathematics Higher

Practice Papers
For SQA Exams

Exam D
Higher
Paper 2

You are allowed 1 hour, 10 minutes to complete this paper.

You may use a calculator.

Full marks will only be awarded where your answer includes relevant working.

You will not receive any marks for answers derived from scale drawings.

Leckie × Leckie
Scotland's leading educational publishers

FORMULAE LIST

Trigonometric formulae

$$\sin(A \pm B) = \sin A \cos B \pm \cos A \sin B$$
$$\cos(A \pm B) = \cos A \cos B \mp \sin A \sin B$$
$$\sin 2A = 2\sin A \cos A$$
$$\cos 2A = \cos^2 A - \sin^2 A$$
$$= 2\cos^2 A - 1$$
$$= 1 - 2\sin^2 A$$

Circle

The equation $x^2 + y^2 + 2gx + 2fy + c = 0$ represents a circle with centre $(-g, -f)$ and radius $\sqrt{g^2 + f^2 - c}$.

The equation $(x - a)^2 + (y - b)^2 = r^2$ represents a circle with centre (a, b) and radius r.

Table of standard integrals

$f(x)$	$\int f(x)\,dx$
$\sin ax$	$-\frac{1}{a}\cos ax + C$
$\cos ax$	$\frac{1}{a}\sin ax + C$

Table of standard derivatives

$f(x)$	$f'(x)$
$\sin ax$	$a \cos ax$
$\cos ax$	$-a \sin ax$

Scalar Product $\boldsymbol{a} \cdot \boldsymbol{b} = |\boldsymbol{a}|\,|\boldsymbol{b}| \cos \theta$, where θ is the angle between $\boldsymbol{a}$ and $\boldsymbol{b}$

or $\boldsymbol{a} \cdot \boldsymbol{b} = a_1b_1 + a_2b_2 + a_3b_3$ where $\boldsymbol{a} = \begin{pmatrix} a_1 \\ a_2 \\ a_3 \end{pmatrix}$ and $\boldsymbol{b} = \begin{pmatrix} b_1 \\ b_2 \\ b_3 \end{pmatrix}$.

Marks

1. (*a*) Express $2\sin x° - \cos x°$ in the form $k \sin (x - a)°$ where $k > 0$ and $0 < a < 360$. **4**

(*b*) Hence find algebraically the values between 0 and 360 for which $2\sin x° - \cos x° = \frac{\sqrt{5}}{2}$. **4**

2. The diagram shows three identical cuboids stacked on top of each other and placed on the coordinate axes. Two edges of the bottom cuboid are along the x-axis and y-axis as shown.

P is the point (10, 4, 9)

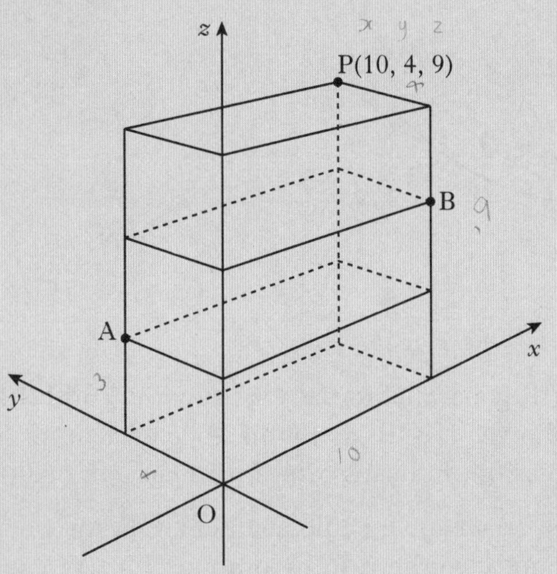

(*a*) State the coordinates of vertices A and B as shown in the diagram. **2**

(*b*) Express $\overrightarrow{BA}$ and $\overrightarrow{BP}$ in component form. **2**

(*c*) Calculate the size of angle ABP. **4**

3. Solve $2\cos 2x + 7\sin x = 0$ for $0 \leq x < 2\pi$. **5**

4. Find the equation of the tangent to the curve with equation $y = (2 - 3x)^{\frac{4}{3}}$ at the point where $x = -2$. **5**

Marks

5. The two curves shown in the diagram have equations $y = 2x^3$ and $y = x^2$ and intersect at the point P.

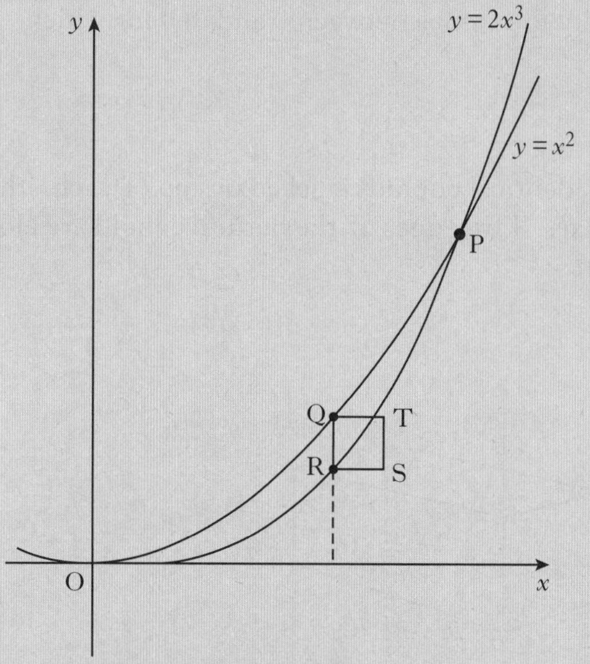

(*a*) Find the x-coordinate of the point P. **1**

(*b*) (i) The line segment QR is parallel to the y-axis, with Q and R lying on the two curves as shown. If QR is at a distance of x units from the y-axis, find an expression, in terms of x, for the length of QR.

(ii) A square QRST is drawn using line segment QR for one side as shown in the diagram. Use the result from part (*b*) (i) to show that the area, A, of the square QRST is given by $A(x) = 4x^6 - 4x^5 + x^4$. **2**

(*c*) Find the maximum area of square QRST for $0 < x < \frac{1}{2}$. **6**

6. Relative to a suitable set of axes the diagram shows circles C_1 and C_2 with centres Q and R respectively. Circle C_1 has equation $x^2 + y^2 - 4x - 2y - 15 = 0$. The line l has equation $y = 2x + 7$.

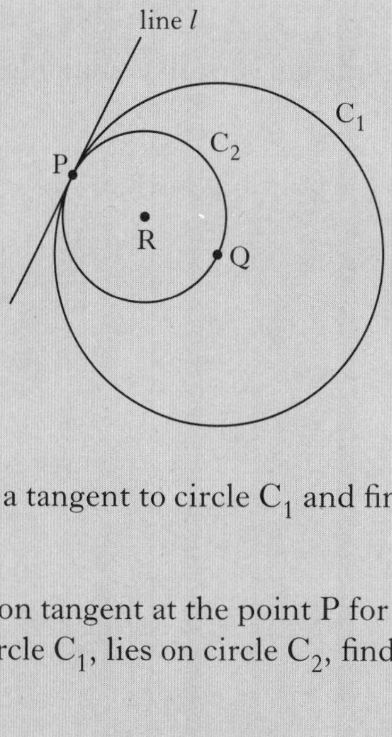

(*a*) Show that line l is a tangent to circle C_1 and find the coordinates of P, the point of contact. **5**

(*b*) If line l is a common tangent at the point P for both circles C_1 and C_2 and Q, the centre of circle C_1, lies on circle C_2, find the equation of circle C_2. **6**

Marks

7. The diagram shows a sketch of the graphs of

$y = 1 - \frac{1}{\sqrt{2x-1}}$ and $y = -\frac{1}{15}x + 1$.

The two graphs intersect at the point A where $x=5$. The two graphs have x-intercepts at $x = 1$ and $x = 15$ as shown.

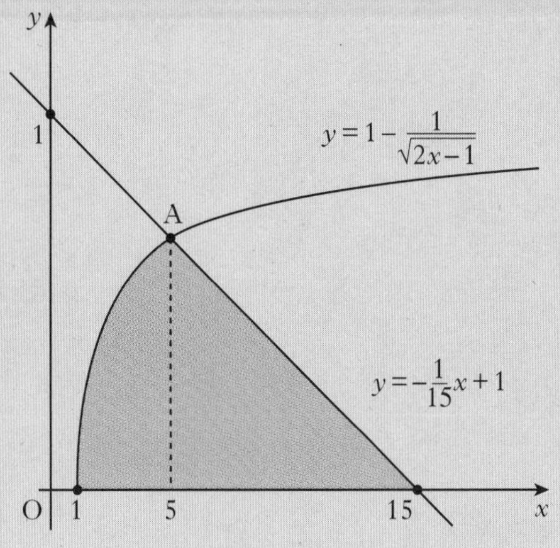

Calculate the shaded area shown in the diagram. **8**

8. (*a*) If $\log_{\sqrt{a}} b = 2c$ show that $\log_a b = c$. **2**

(*b*) Hence show that

$\log_5 7 - \log_{25} 7 = \log_{25} 7$. **3**

[End of question paper]

Practice Exam E

Mathematics Higher

Practice Papers
For SQA Exams

Exam E
Higher
Paper 1
Non-calculator

You are allowed 1 hour, 30 minutes to complete this paper.

You must not use a calculator.

Full marks will only be awarded where your answers include relevant working.

You will not receive any marks for answers derived from scale drawings.

Leckie × Leckie
Scotland's leading educational publishers

FORMULAE LIST

Trigonometric formulae

$$\sin(A \pm B) = \sin A \cos B \pm \cos A \sin B$$
$$\cos(A \pm B) = \cos A \cos B \mp \sin A \sin B$$
$$\sin 2A = 2\sin A \cos A$$
$$\cos 2A = \cos^2 A - \sin^2 A$$
$$= 2\cos^2 A - 1$$
$$= 1 - 2\sin^2 A$$

Circle

The equation $x^2 + y^2 + 2gx + 2fy + c = 0$ represents a circle with centre $(-g, -f)$ and radius $\sqrt{g^2 + f^2 - c}$.

The equation $(x - a)^2 + (y - b)^2 = r^2$ represents a circle with centre (a, b) and radius r.

Table of standard integrals

$f(x)$	$\int f(x)\,dx$
$\sin ax$	$-\frac{1}{a}\cos ax + C$
$\cos ax$	$\frac{1}{a}\sin ax + C$

Table of standard derivatives

$f(x)$	$f'(x)$
$\sin ax$	$a \cos ax$
$\cos ax$	$-a \sin ax$

Scalar Product $\boldsymbol{a} \cdot \boldsymbol{b} = |\boldsymbol{a}||\boldsymbol{b}| \cos\theta$, where θ is the angle between $\boldsymbol{a}$ and $\boldsymbol{b}$

or $\boldsymbol{a} \cdot \boldsymbol{b} = a_1b_1 + a_2b_2 + a_3b_3$ where $\boldsymbol{a} = \begin{pmatrix} a_1 \\ a_2 \\ a_3 \end{pmatrix}$ and $\boldsymbol{b} = \begin{pmatrix} b_1 \\ b_2 \\ b_3 \end{pmatrix}$.

SECTION A

1. A circle has equation $x^2 + y^2 - 2x + 4y + 1 = 0$. What is the radius of this circle?

A 1

B 2

C $\sqrt{19}$

D 6

2. A sequence is defined by $u_{n+1} = 5 - 2u_n$ with $u_1 = 3$. What is the value of u_3?

A −3

B 4

C 7

D 9

3. What is the distance between the points P(−1, 3) and Q(−2, 0)?

A $\sqrt{8}$

B $\sqrt{10}$

C $\sqrt{18}$

D $\sqrt{26}$

4. Triangle ABC has vertices A(−1, 0), B(1, 4) and C(5, −2). What is the gradient of a line that is parallel to side AB?

A −2

B $-\frac{4}{5}$

C $-\frac{1}{2}$

D 2

5. A curve has equation $y = 3x - 2x^3$. What is the gradient of the tangent at the point (2, −10)?

A −21

B −10

C −9

D −5

6. The function f is defined by $f(x) = \frac{2}{3x^2}$, $x \neq 0$.
Find $f'(x)$.

A $\frac{1}{3x}$

B $-\frac{1}{3x}$

C $\frac{12}{x^3}$

D $-\frac{4}{3x^3}$

7. A sequence is defined by the recurrence relation

$u_{n+1} = 0{\cdot}85u_n + 1{\cdot}5$ and $u_0 = 2{\cdot}5$.

Here are two statements about this sequence

(1) There is a term of this sequence greater than 10.

(2) A limit does not exist for this sequence.

Which of the following is true?

A Neither statement is correct.

B Only statement (1) is correct.

C Only statement (2) is correct.

D Both statements are correct.

8. If the exact value of $\tan x$ is $\frac{1}{\sqrt{2}}$, where $0 \leq x \leq \frac{\pi}{2}$, find the exact value of $\sin 2x$.

A $\frac{\sqrt{2}}{9}$

B $\frac{2\sqrt{2}}{3\sqrt{3}}$

C $\frac{2\sqrt{2}}{3}$

D $\frac{2}{\sqrt{3}}$

9. Which of the following graphs could have equation $y = \log_3(x - 1)$?

A

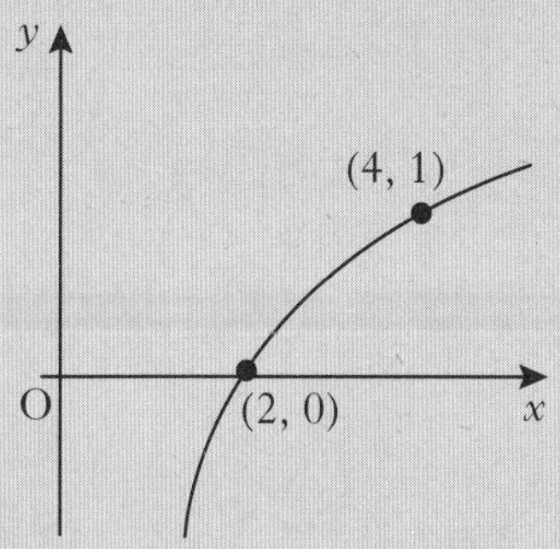

B

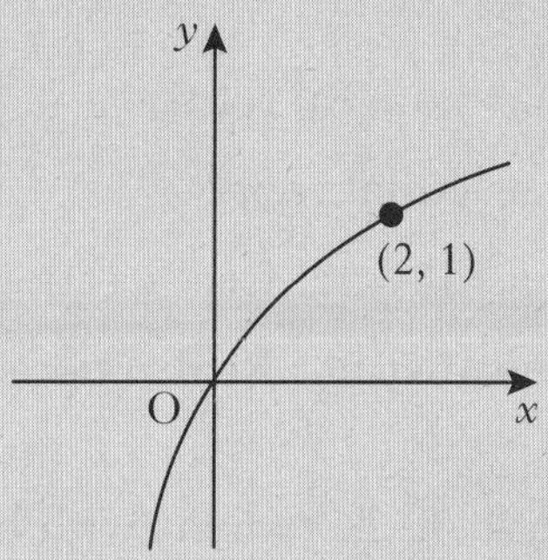

C

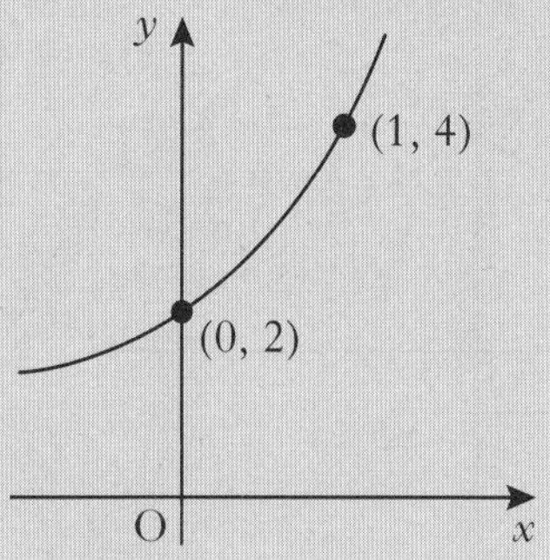

D

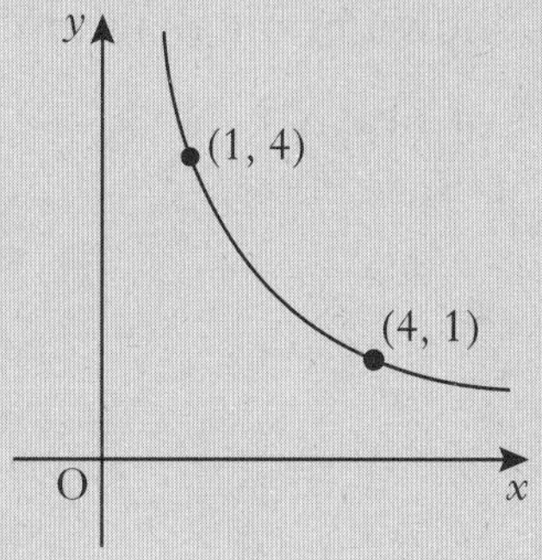

10. How many solutions does the equation $2\sin x(2\cos x - 3) = 0$ have in the interval $0 \leq x < 2\pi$?

A 1

B 2

C 3

D 4

11. The line with equation $y = -x$ intersects the circle with equation $x^2 + y^2 = 4$ at the points $P(x_P, y_P)$ and $Q(x_Q, y_Q)$. What are the values of x_P and x_Q?

	x_P	x_Q
A	0	0
B	$\frac{1}{\sqrt{2}}$	$-\frac{1}{\sqrt{2}}$
C	1	-1
D	$\sqrt{2}$	$-\sqrt{2}$

12. Functions f and g are defined by

$$f(x) = \sqrt{2}\sin\frac{1}{2}x + 2$$

and $g(x) = k$

where x is a Real number and k is a constant.
For which of these ranges for k has the equation $f(x) = g(x)$ no Real solution?

A $k < 2$

B $-\sqrt{2} < k < \sqrt{2}$

C $2 - \sqrt{2} < k < 2 + \sqrt{2}$

D $k > 2 + \sqrt{2}$

13. Which one of the following statements is true for the equation $9m^2 - 3m - 2 = 0$?

A The equation has no Real roots.

B The equation has equal roots.

C The equation has distinct Real irrational roots.

D The equation has distinct Real rational roots.

14. Line L makes an angle of $\frac{\pi}{3}$ radians with both the y-axis and line M as shown in the diagram.

What is the gradient of line M?

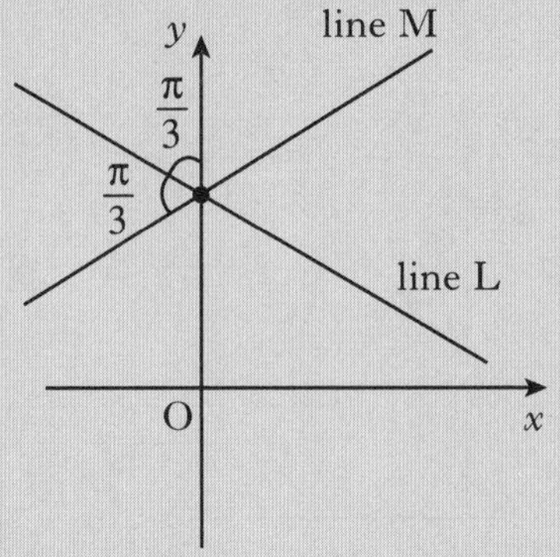

A $\frac{1}{2}$

B $\frac{1}{\sqrt{3}}$

C $\frac{1}{\sqrt{2}}$

D $\frac{\sqrt{3}}{2}$

15. R and θ are given by:

$$R\sin\theta = \sqrt{3}$$
$$R\cos\theta = \sqrt{3}$$

Where $R > 0$ and $0 \leq \theta < \frac{\pi}{2}$.

What are the values of R and θ?

	R	θ
A	$\sqrt{6}$	$\frac{\pi}{4}$
B	$\sqrt{6}$	$\frac{\pi}{3}$
C	$3\sqrt{2}$	$\frac{\pi}{4}$
D	$3\sqrt{2}$	$\frac{\pi}{3}$

16. A function f is given by $f(x) = \dfrac{2}{\sqrt{1-3x}}$ on a suitable domain.

Find $f'(x)$.

A $3(1-3x)^{-\frac{3}{2}}$

B $(1-3x)^{-\frac{1}{2}}$

C $-\frac{4}{3}(1-3x)^{\frac{1}{2}}$

D $-3x(1-3x)^{-\frac{3}{2}}$

17. The diagram shows part of the graph $y = -x^2$.

Which of the following gives the shaded area?

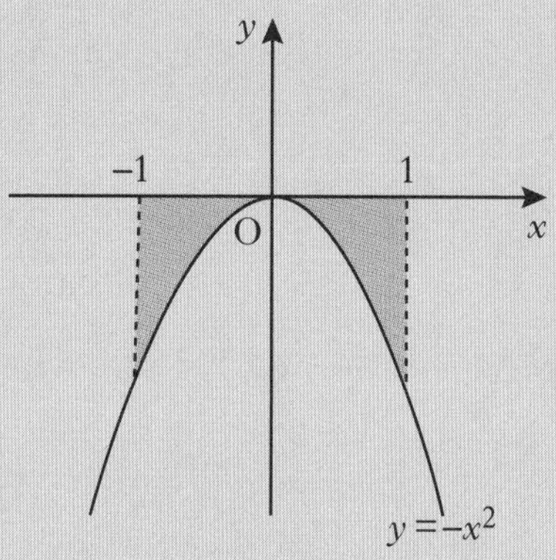

A $-2\left[-\dfrac{x^3}{3}\right]_0^1$

B $\left[-\dfrac{x^3}{3}\right]_{-1}^1$

C $-2[-2x]_0^1$

D $[-2x]_{-1}^1$

18. If $\boldsymbol{v}$ and $\boldsymbol{u}$ are perpendicular unit vectors, which of the following statements is true?

A $\boldsymbol{v} \cdot \boldsymbol{u} = 1$

B $|\boldsymbol{v}| = 1$ and $|\boldsymbol{u}| = 1$ and $\dfrac{\boldsymbol{v} \cdot \boldsymbol{u}}{|\boldsymbol{v}||\boldsymbol{u}|} = 0$

C $|\boldsymbol{v} - \boldsymbol{u}| = 0$

D $|\boldsymbol{v}| = 1$ and $|\boldsymbol{u}| = 1$ and $\dfrac{\boldsymbol{v} \cdot \boldsymbol{u}}{|\boldsymbol{v}||\boldsymbol{u}|} = 1$

19.

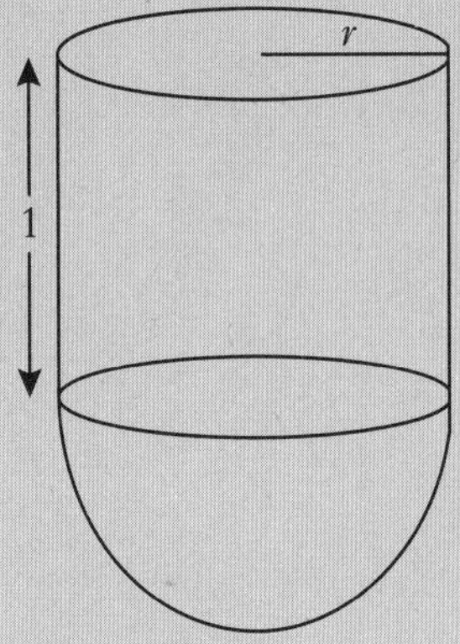

The Volume of this solid is given by: $V(r) = \frac{2}{3}\pi r^3 + \pi r^2$.

What is $V'\left(\frac{1}{2}\right)$?

A $\frac{5\pi}{96}$

B $\frac{5\pi}{6}$

C $\frac{3\pi}{2}$

D 2π

20. What is the solution of $1 < 4t^2$, where t is a Real number?

A $t > -\frac{1}{2}$

B $-\frac{1}{2} \leq t \leq \frac{1}{2}$

C $t < -\frac{1}{2}$ or $t > \frac{1}{2}$

D $t < -2$ or $t > 2$

[End of section A]

SECTION B

Marks

21. ABC is a right-angled triangle as shown in the diagram, with vertices A(1, −2, −k), B(k, k, 0) and C(4, −3, 3 − k).

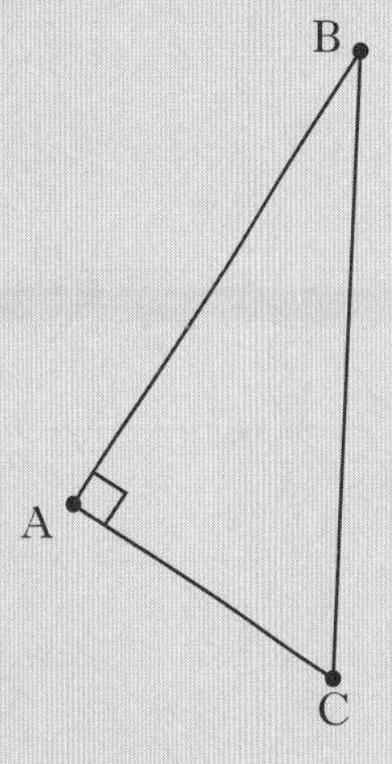

(a) Find the value of k. **4**

D is the point (13, −6, 11).

(b) Show that A, C and D are collinear and find the ratio in which C divides AD. **4**

22. Triangle PQR has vertices P(−3, 1), Q(3, 5) and R(1, −3). PM is a median. The line through M parallel to altitude QT meets side PR at the point N as shown.

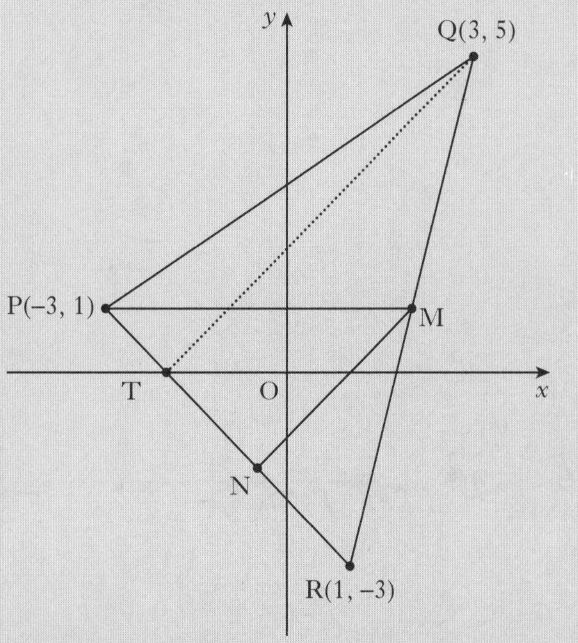

(a) State the coordinates of M. **1**

(b) Find the equation of line MN. **3**

(c) Find the coordinates of N. **4**

Marks

23. (*a*)

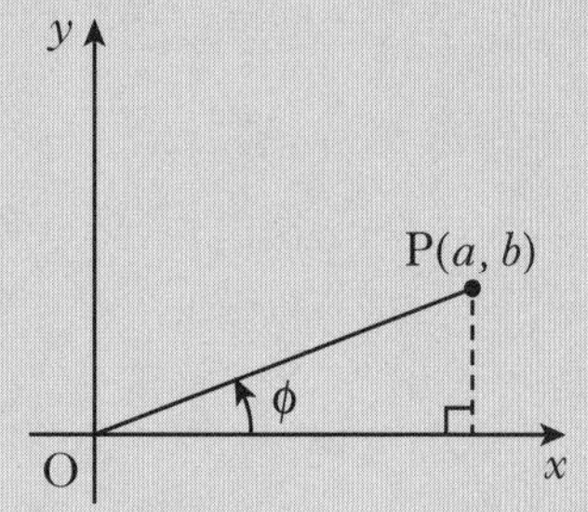

P is point (a, b). Line OP makes an angle of ϕ with the x-axis as shown.

(i) Show that $\cos\phi = \dfrac{a}{\sqrt{a^2+b^2}}$. **2**

(ii) Find a similar expression for $\sin\phi$. **1**

(*b*)

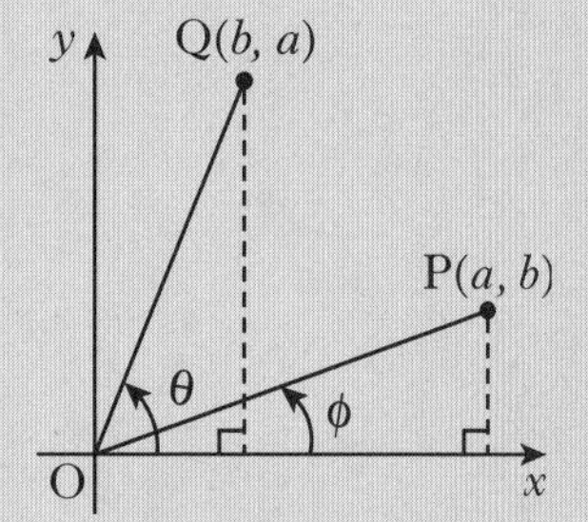

OQ makes an angle of θ with the x-axis, where Q is the point (b, a).

(i) Show that $\cos(\theta - \phi) = \dfrac{2ab}{a^2+b^2}$. **4**

(ii) Find a similar simplified expression for $\sin(\theta - \phi)$. **2**

24. The diagram shows a sketch of the function $y = f(x)$.

(*a*) Sketch the graph of

$$y = f\left(\frac{1}{2}x\right).$$

2

(*b*) On a separate diagram sketch the graph of $y = 2f\left(\frac{1}{2}x\right) + 1$. **3**

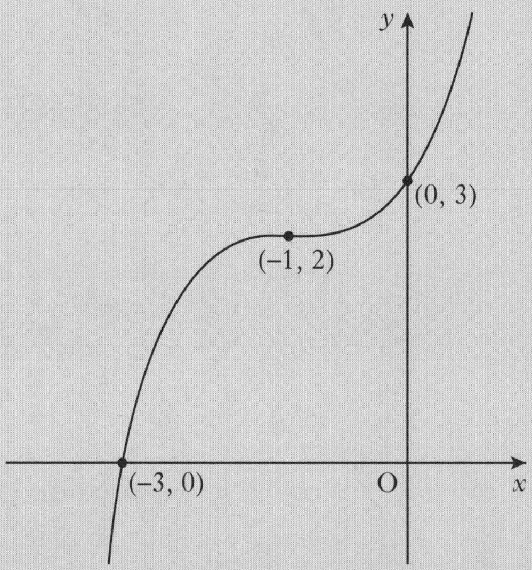

[End of section B]

[End of question paper]

Mathematics Higher

Practice Papers
For SQA Exams

Exam E
Higher
Paper 2

You are allowed 1 hour, 10 minutes to complete this paper.

You may use a calculator.

Full marks will only be awarded where your answer includes relevant working.

You will not receive any marks for answers derived from scale drawings.

Leckie × Leckie
Scotland's leading educational publishers

FORMULAE LIST

Trigonometric formulae

$$\sin(A \pm B) = \sin A \cos B \pm \cos A \sin B$$
$$\cos(A \pm B) = \cos A \cos B \mp \sin A \sin B$$
$$\sin 2A = 2\sin A \cos A$$
$$\begin{aligned}\cos 2A &= \cos^2 A - \sin^2 A \\ &= 2\cos^2 A - 1 \\ &= 1 - 2\sin^2 A\end{aligned}$$

Circle

The equation $x^2 + y^2 + 2gx + 2fy + c = 0$ represents a circle with centre $(-g, -f)$ and radius $\sqrt{g^2 + f^2 - c}$.

The equation $(x - a)^2 + (y - b)^2 = r^2$ represents a circle with centre (a, b) and radius r.

Table of standard integrals

$f(x)$	$\int f(x)\,dx$
$\sin ax$	$-\frac{1}{a}\cos ax + C$
$\cos ax$	$\frac{1}{a}\sin ax + C$

Table of standard derivatives

$f(x)$	$f'(x)$
$\sin ax$	$a \cos ax$
$\cos ax$	$-a \sin ax$

Scalar Product $\boldsymbol{a}.\boldsymbol{b} = |\boldsymbol{a}||\boldsymbol{b}|\cos\theta$, where θ is the angle between $\boldsymbol{a}$ and $\boldsymbol{b}$

or $\boldsymbol{a}.\boldsymbol{b} = a_1b_1 + a_2b_2 + a_3b_3$ where $\boldsymbol{a} = \begin{pmatrix} a_1 \\ a_2 \\ a_3 \end{pmatrix}$ and $\boldsymbol{b} = \begin{pmatrix} b_1 \\ b_2 \\ b_3 \end{pmatrix}$.

Marks

1. (*a*) Show that $x + 3$ is a factor of $f(x) = 6x^3 + 13x^2 - 14x + 3$. **2**

(*b*) Hence factorise $f(x)$ fully. **3**

2. A curve has equation $y = 2x^3 - x^2 + 1$.
Find the coordinates of the stationary points on the curve and determine their nature. **8**

3. The functions f and g are defined on a suitable domain by $f(x) = \dfrac{2}{x+1}$ and $g(x) = 2x + 1$.

(*a*) Prove that $f(g(x)) = \dfrac{1}{2}f(x)$. **4**

(*b*) Find a simplified expression for $\dfrac{g'(x)}{f(x)}$. **2**

4. The graphs $y = f(x) = \sin ax + b$ and $y = g(x) = \sin cx + d$ are shown in the diagram for $0 \leq x \leq 2\pi$.

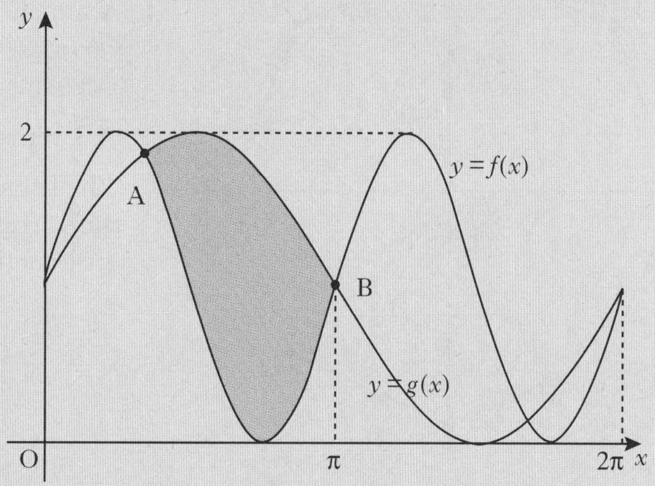

(*a*) Write down the values of a, b, c and d. **1**

(*b*) In the interval $0 < x \leq \pi$ the two curves intersect at points A and B as shown. B is the point $(\pi, 1)$. Calculate the exact value of the x-coordinate of point A. **4**

(*c*) Calculate the exact value of the shaded area shown in the diagram. **6**

5. (*a*) The line with equation $2y = x - 2$ is a tangent to the circle $x^2 + y^2 + 6x - 20y - 16 = 0$.

A is the point $(-8, 0)$. Chord AB is parallel to the tangent.

Find the coordinates of B. **5**

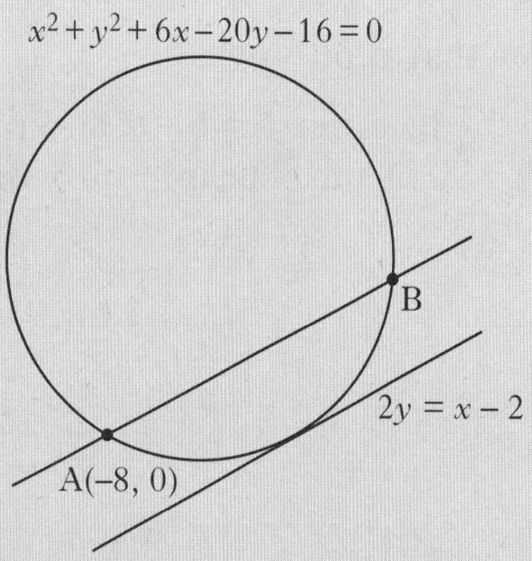

(*b*) (i) Find the equation of the circle with AB as diameter. **3**

(ii) Hence find the length of the chord created by the intersection of this circle with the x-axis. **2**

6. (*a*) Simplify $\dfrac{2x^2 - 7x + 6}{x^2 - 4}$. **2**

(*b*) Solve $\log_3(2x^2 - 7x + 6) - \log_3(x^2 - 4) = 2$. **3**

Marks

7. The amount, A kg, of a radioactive substance after t years is given by $A = A_0e^{-kt}$ where A_0 kg is the initial amount of the substance and k is a constant. After 500 years, a sample of a certain isotope of radium has decayed to 80·4% of its initial mass.

(*a*) Find the value of constant k to 3 significant figures for this particular isotope. **3**

The half-life of a substance is the length of time in which half the substance decays.

(*b*) Find the half-life of this particular isotope of radium. **2**

8.

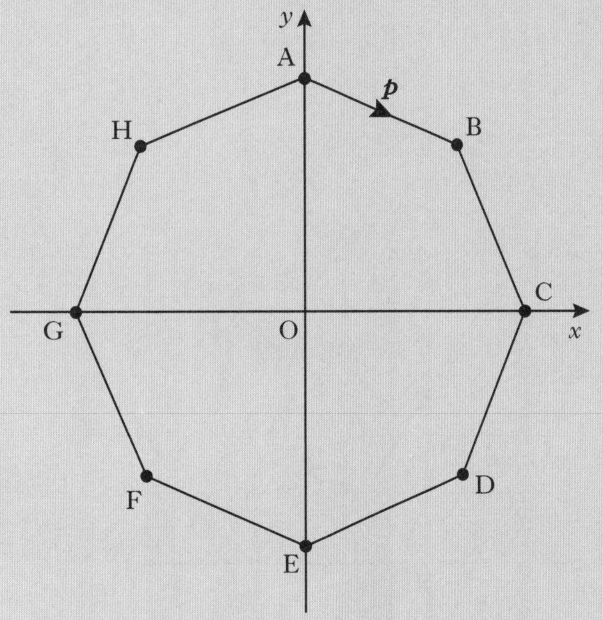

The diagram shows a regular octagon ABCDEFGH with centre at the origin. Vertices A and E lie on the y-axis and vertices C and G lie on the x-axis as shown.

$\overrightarrow{AB}$ represents vector $\boldsymbol{p}$.

The position vectors of all the vertices of the octagon are unit vectors.

(*a*) Calculate the exact value of $\boldsymbol{a}.\boldsymbol{b}$ where $\boldsymbol{a}$ and $\boldsymbol{b}$ are the position vectors of vertices A and B respectively. **2**

(*b*) Show that $\boldsymbol{p}.\boldsymbol{p} = |\boldsymbol{p}|^2$. **2**

(*c*) Use the fact that $\boldsymbol{p} = \boldsymbol{b} - \boldsymbol{a}$ and the results (*a*) and (*b*) above to show that each side of the octagon is of length $\sqrt{2-\sqrt{2}}$ units. **6**

[End of question paper]

Practice Exam F

Mathematics Higher

Practice Papers
For SQA Exams

Exam F
Higher
Paper 1
Non-calculator

You are allowed 1 hour, 30 minutes to complete this paper.

You must **not** use a calculator.

Full marks will only be awarded where your answers include relevant working.

You will not receive any marks for answers derived from scale drawings.

Leckie × Leckie
Scotland's leading educational publishers

FORMULAE LIST

Trigonometric formulae

$$\sin(A \pm B) = \sin A \cos B \pm \cos A \sin B$$
$$\cos(A \pm B) = \cos A \cos B \mp \sin A \sin B$$
$$\sin 2A = 2\sin A \cos A$$
$$\cos 2A = \cos^2 A - \sin^2 A$$
$$= 2\cos^2 A - 1$$
$$= 1 - 2\sin^2 A$$

Circle

The equation $x^2 + y^2 + 2gx + 2fy + c = 0$ represents a circle with centre $(-g, -f)$ and radius $\sqrt{g^2 + f^2 - c}$.

The equation $(x - a)^2 + (y - b)^2 = r^2$ represents a circle with centre (a, b) and radius r.

Table of standard integrals

$f(x)$	$\int f(x)\,dx$
$\sin ax$	$-\frac{1}{a}\cos ax + C$
$\cos ax$	$\frac{1}{a}\sin ax + C$

Table of standard derivatives

$f(x)$	$f'(x)$
$\sin ax$	$a \cos ax$
$\cos ax$	$-a \sin ax$

Scalar Product $\boldsymbol{a} \cdot \boldsymbol{b} = |\boldsymbol{a}||\boldsymbol{b}| \cos\theta$, where θ is the angle between $\boldsymbol{a}$ and $\boldsymbol{b}$

or $\boldsymbol{a} \cdot \boldsymbol{b} = a_1b_1 + a_2b_2 + a_3b_3$ where $\boldsymbol{a} = \begin{pmatrix} a_1 \\ a_2 \\ a_3 \end{pmatrix}$ and $\boldsymbol{b} = \begin{pmatrix} b_1 \\ b_2 \\ b_3 \end{pmatrix}$.

SECTION A

1. Two functions f and g are given by $f(x) = 2x^2$ and $g(x) = 3 - x$. Find an expression for $g(f(x))$.

A $3 - 2x^2$

B $3 - 2x^3$

C $6x^2 - 2x^3$

D $18 - 12x + 2x^2$

2. The equation of line L is $3y - x = 4$ and the equation of line M is $y + 3x = 5$.

Which of the following is a true statement?

A Lines L and M are parallel.

B Lines L and M are not parallel, not perpendicular and have positive gradients.

C Lines L and M are perpendicular.

D Lines L and M are not parallel, not perpendicular and one line has a positive gradient and one has a negative gradient.

3. A circle has equation $x^2 + y^2 = 6x - 4y - 9$. What is the radius of this circle?

A 2

B $\sqrt{10}$

C $\sqrt{61}$

D 22

4. What is the distance between the points $(2, -3)$ and $(-4, 1)$?

A $2\sqrt{2}$

B $2\sqrt{5}$

C $5\sqrt{2}$

D $2\sqrt{13}$

5. Find $f'(x)$ where $f(x) = \dfrac{1}{\sin x}$.

A $-\dfrac{\cos x}{x^2}$

B $-\dfrac{1}{\sin^2 x}$

C $-\dfrac{\cos x}{\sin^2 x}$

D $\dfrac{1}{\cos x}$

6. What is the minimum point on the graph $y = (2x - 1)^2 - 3$?

A $\left(-\frac{1}{2}, 3\right)$

B $(0, -3)$

C $(0, -2)$

D $\left(\frac{1}{2}, -3\right)$

7. A sequence is generated by the recurrence relation $u_{n+1} = ku_n + 8$. What is the value of k that gives this sequence a limit of 24 as $n \to \infty$?

A $-\frac{1}{3}$

B $\frac{1}{2}$

C $\frac{2}{3}$

D 3

8. Function f is given by $f(x) = \frac{2}{1 - x^2}$.

What is a suitable domain for the function f?

A All Real numbers.

B All Real numbers apart from -1.

C All Real numbers apart from 1.

D All Real numbers apart from 1 and -1.

9. Find the equation of the circle that has a diameter with end points $(-1, 0)$ and $(5, 8)$.

A $(x - 2)^2 + (y - 4)^2 = 25$

B $(x - 2)^2 + (y - 4)^2 = 100$

C $(x - 3)^2 + (y - 4)^2 = 20$

D $(x + 1)^2 + y^2 = 100$

10. If $\sin\theta = \frac{5}{13}$ and $0 < \theta < \frac{\pi}{2}$, what is the exact value of $\sin 2\theta$?

A $\frac{2}{13}$

B $\frac{5}{13}$

C $\frac{119}{169}$

D $\frac{120}{169}$

11. The diagram shows an isosceles triangle PQR with an altitude drawn. Lengths and angles are as shown. Express $\cos 2a°$ in terms of d and e.

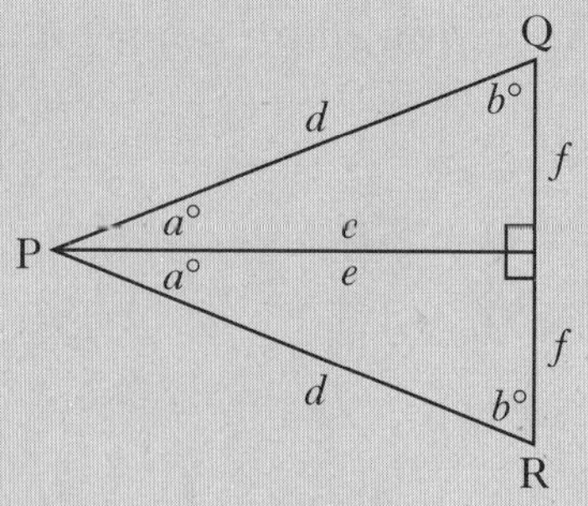

A $\dfrac{2e^2}{d^2}$

B $\dfrac{2e^2 - d^2}{d^2}$

C $\dfrac{2e}{d}$

D $\dfrac{2e\sqrt{d^2 - e^2}}{d^2}$

12. Find $\int (3 - 2x)^4\, dx$

A $-\frac{1}{10}(3 - 2x)^5 + C$

B $-\frac{2}{5}(3 - 2x)^5 + C$

C $-8(3 - 2x)^4 + C$

D $\frac{1}{10}(3 - 2x)^5 + C$

13. The diagram shows the graphs $y = x^2 - 4$ and $y = 4 - x^2$. Which of the following does not give the shaded area?

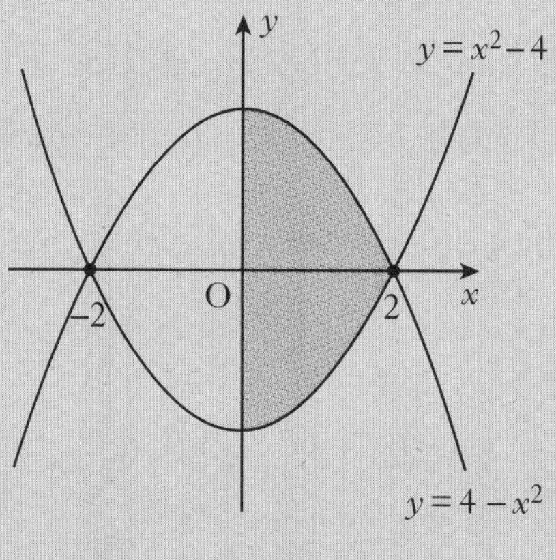

A $\int_0^2 (4 - x^2)\, dx$

B $\int_{-2}^2 (4 - x^2)\, dx$

C $\int_0^2 (4 - x^2)\, dx - \int_0^2 (x^2 - 4)\, dx$

D $\int_0^2 (4 - x^2)\, dx + \int_0^2 (x^2 - 4)\, dx$

14. Which of the following shows part of the graph $y = \log_5 2x$?

A

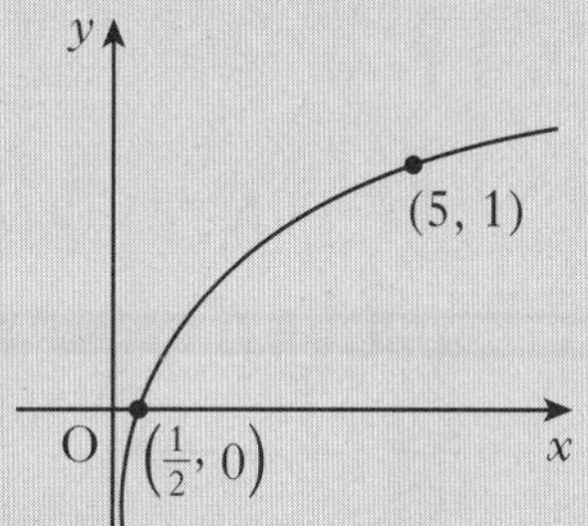

B

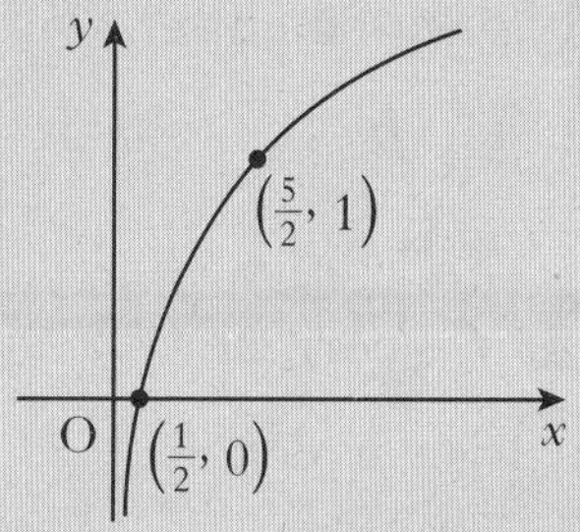

C

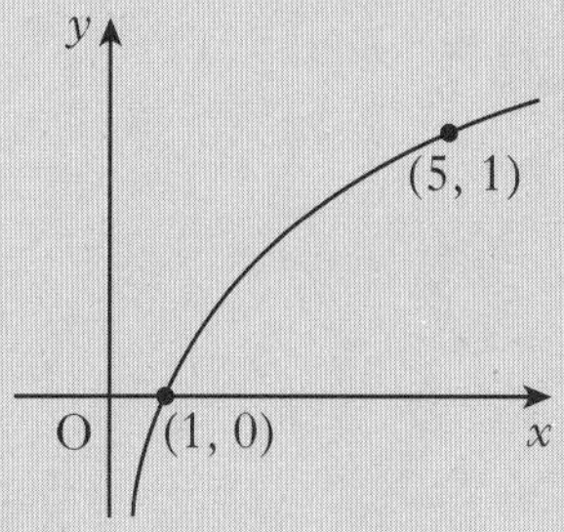

D

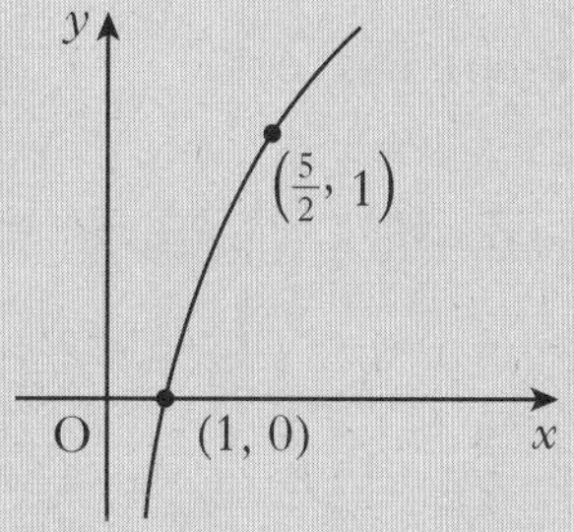

15. Find the exact value of $\log_3\left(\frac{1}{3}\right)$.

A -1

B 0

C $\frac{1}{2}$

D 1

16. The two vectors $\begin{pmatrix} m \\ 1 \\ -1 \end{pmatrix}$ and $\begin{pmatrix} 1 \\ 2 \\ -1 \end{pmatrix}$ are perpendicular. Find the value of m.

A -3

B -2

C -1

D 1

17. Solve $\sin 2x = 0$ for $\frac{\pi}{2} < x \leq \frac{3\pi}{2}$.

A $x = 0, \frac{\pi}{2}, \pi, \frac{3\pi}{2}$

B $x = \frac{\pi}{2}, \pi, \frac{3\pi}{2}$

C $x = \pi, \frac{3\pi}{2}$

D $x = \frac{3\pi}{2}$

18. Three unit vectors $\boldsymbol{p}$, $\boldsymbol{q}$ and $\boldsymbol{r}$ are represented by the sides of an equilateral triangle as shown in the diagram. Here are two statements:

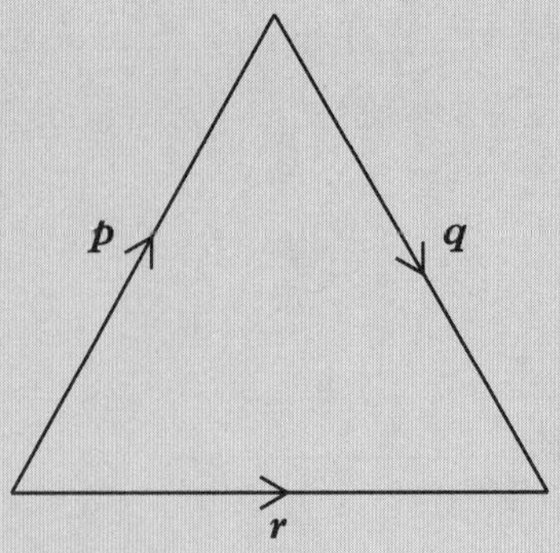

I $\boldsymbol{p}\,.\,(\boldsymbol{q}+\boldsymbol{r})=0$ II $\boldsymbol{p}\,.\,(\boldsymbol{q}-\boldsymbol{r})=1$

Which of the following is true?

A Neither statement is correct.

B Only statement I is correct.

C Only statement II is correct.

D Both statements are correct.

19. What is the solution to the equation

$2\cos^2 x = 1$ in the interval $0 \le x \le 2\pi$?

A $\frac{\pi}{8}, \frac{3\pi}{8}, \frac{5\pi}{8}, \frac{7\pi}{8}, \frac{9\pi}{8}, \frac{11\pi}{8}, \frac{13\pi}{8}, \frac{15\pi}{8}$

B $\frac{2\pi}{3}, \frac{4\pi}{3}$

C $\frac{\pi}{4}, \frac{3\pi}{4}, \frac{5\pi}{4}, \frac{7\pi}{4}$

D $\frac{\pi}{6}, \frac{5\pi}{6}$

20. If $p^{(q^p)} = q$ which of the following is not equal to q^p?

A $\frac{\log_e q}{\log_e p}$

B $\log_{10}(q-p)$

C $\log_p q$

D $\frac{1}{\log_q p}$

[End of section A]

SECTION B

Marks

21.

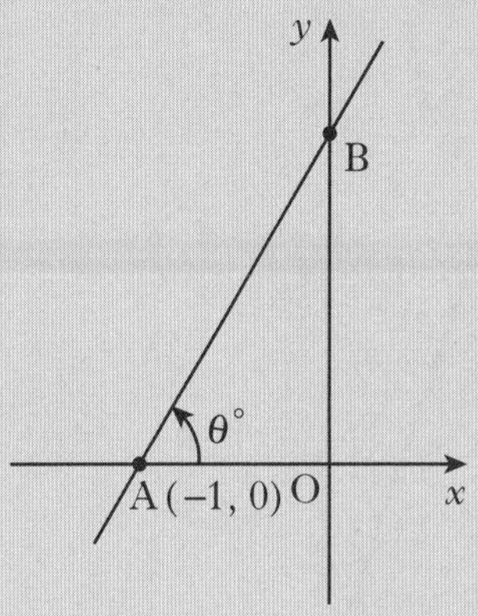

$\sin\theta^\circ$	$\frac{\sqrt{6}}{3}$
$\cos\theta^\circ$	$\frac{\sqrt{3}}{3}$
$\tan\theta^\circ$	$\sqrt{2}$

The line AB makes an angle of θ° with the x-axis as shown in the diagram. A is the point (–1, 0). The table gives information about angle θ°.

Use the information given to find the equation of the line AB. **3**

22. A sequence is defined by $u_{n+1} = \frac{1}{k}u_n + 1$ with $u_0 = k^2$.

(*a*) Express u_1 and u_2 in terms of k in simplified form. **2**

(*b*) Given that $u_2 = 3k$ show that it is not possible for any resulting sequence to have a limit. **3**

23.

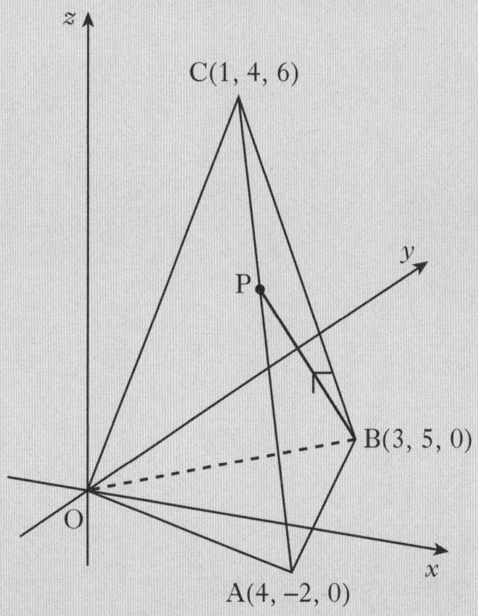

OABC is a tetrahedron. A is the point (4, –2, 0), B is (3, 5, 0) and C is (1, 4, 6). P divides AC in the ratio 2:1.

(*a*) Find the coordinates of P. **4**

(*b*) Express $\overrightarrow{BP}$ in terms of the unit vectors $\boldsymbol{i}$, $\boldsymbol{j}$ and $\boldsymbol{k}$. **1**

24. Express $2(\sqrt{3}\cos x - \sin x)$ in the form $k\cos(x + a)$ where $k > 0$ and $0 \le a < 2\pi$. **4**

25. (*a*) Show that $x = -4$ is a root of $x^3 + 4x^2 - 25x - 100 = 0$ and hence factorise $x^3 + 4x^2 - 25x - 100$ fully. **5**

(*b*) Hence, or otherwise, determine the number of points of intersection that the line $y = x + 4$ makes with the curve $y = x^3 + 4x^2 - 24x - 96$. **2**

Marks

26. (*a*) Write down the equation of a circle with centre (0, 5) and radius r units. **1**

(*b*) Find the exact value of r such that $y = 15 - 3x$ is a tangent to this circle. **5**

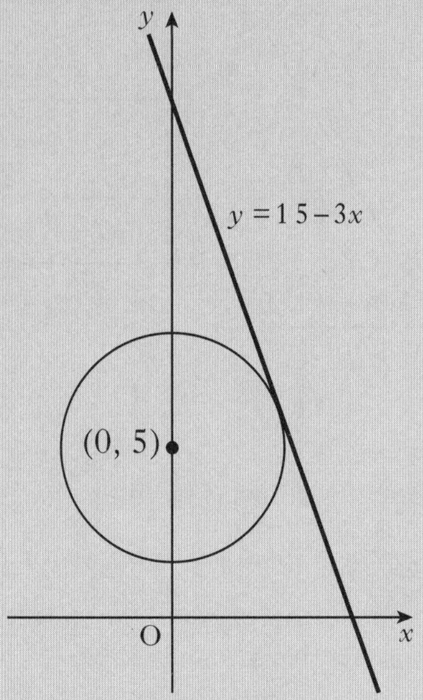

[End of section B]

[End of question paper]

Mathematics Higher

Practice Papers
For SQA Exams

Exam F
Higher
Paper 2

You are allowed 1 hour, 10 minutes to complete this paper.

You may use a calculator.

Full marks will only be awarded where your answer includes relevant working.

You will not receive any marks for answers derived from scale drawings.

Leckie × Leckie
Scotland's leading educational publishers

FORMULAE LIST

Trigonometric formulae

$$\sin(A \pm B) = \sin A \cos B \pm \cos A \sin B$$
$$\cos(A \pm B) = \cos A \cos B \mp \sin A \sin B$$
$$\sin 2A = 2\sin A \cos A$$
$$\cos 2A = \cos^2 A - \sin^2 A$$
$$= 2\cos^2 A - 1$$
$$= 1 - 2\sin^2 A$$

Circle

The equation $x^2 + y^2 + 2gx + 2fy + c = 0$ represents a circle with centre $(-g, -f)$ and radius $\sqrt{g^2 + f^2 - c}$.

The equation $(x - a)^2 + (y - b)^2 = r^2$ represents a circle with centre (a, b) and radius r.

Table of standard integrals

$f(x)$	$\int f(x)\,dx$
$\sin ax$	$-\frac{1}{a}\cos ax + C$
$\cos ax$	$\frac{1}{a}\sin ax + C$

Table of standard derivatives

$f(x)$	$f'(x)$
$\sin ax$	$a \cos ax$
$\cos ax$	$-a \sin ax$

Scalar Product $\quad \boldsymbol{a} \cdot \boldsymbol{b} = |\boldsymbol{a}|\,|\boldsymbol{b}| \cos \theta$, where θ is the angle between $\boldsymbol{a}$ and $\boldsymbol{b}$

or $\quad \boldsymbol{a} \cdot \boldsymbol{b} = a_1b_1 + a_2b_2 + a_3b_3$ where $\boldsymbol{a} = \begin{pmatrix} a_1 \\ a_2 \\ a_3 \end{pmatrix}$ and $\boldsymbol{b} = \begin{pmatrix} b_1 \\ b_2 \\ b_3 \end{pmatrix}$.

Marks

1. 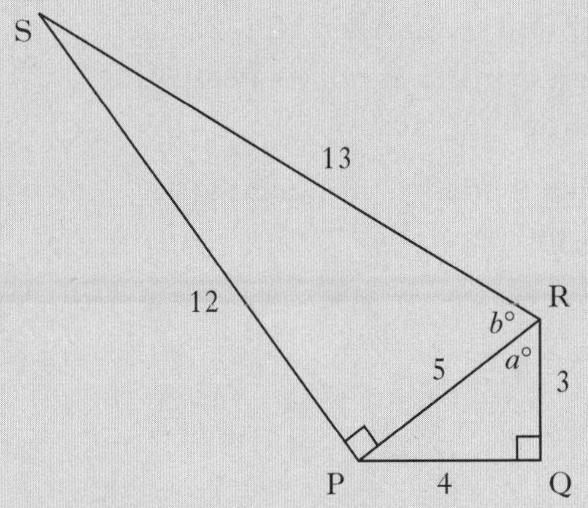

Two right-angled triangles PQR and RPS have lengths as shown in the diagram.

Angle PRQ = $a°$ and angle PRS = $b°$.

(*a*) Show that the exact value of $\cos(a+b)°$ is $-\frac{33}{65}$. **4**

(*b*) Calculate the exact value of $\sin(a+b)°$. **2**

(*c*) Hence calculate the exact value of $\tan(a+b)°$. **1**

2. Find $\int \frac{2-x^5}{x^3}\,dx$. **4**

3. The diagram shows a cuboid surmounted by a pyramid. One of the triangular faces of the pyramid has vertices A(3, 2, 5), B(6, 0, 3) and C(6, 4, 3).

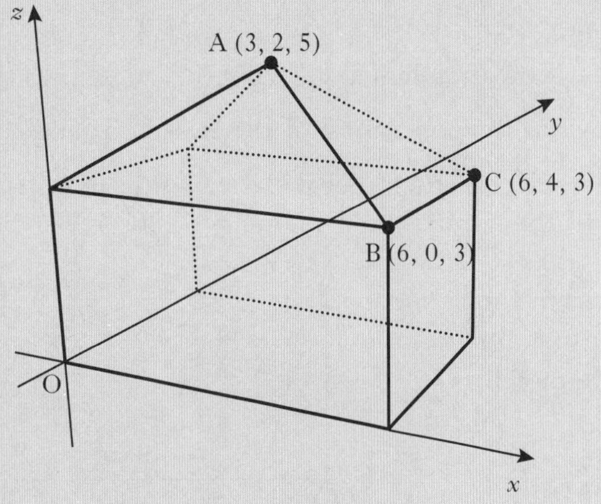

(*a*) Express $\overrightarrow{CA}$ and $\overrightarrow{CB}$ in component form. **2**

(*b*) Calculate the angle between the two edges CA and CB. **5**

4. 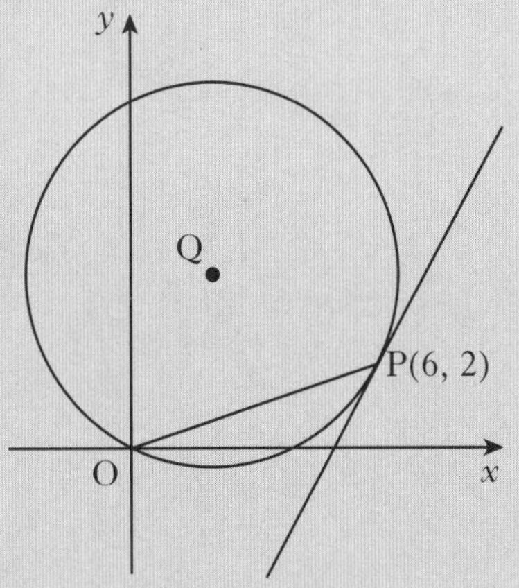

The diagram shows a circle, centre Q, which passes through the origin and the point P(6, 2).

(*a*) Find the equation of the perpendicular bisector of chord OP. **3**

(*b*) The tangent to the circle at P(6, 2) has equation $y - 2x + 10 = 0$. Find the equation of radius QP. **4**

(*c*) Hence find the coordinates of Q. **3**

5. Function f is defined by $f(x) = \frac{2}{3\sqrt{x}}$, where $x > 0$. The diagram shows part of the graph of $y = f(x)$.

Find the equation of the tangent at the point A where $x = 1$. **6**

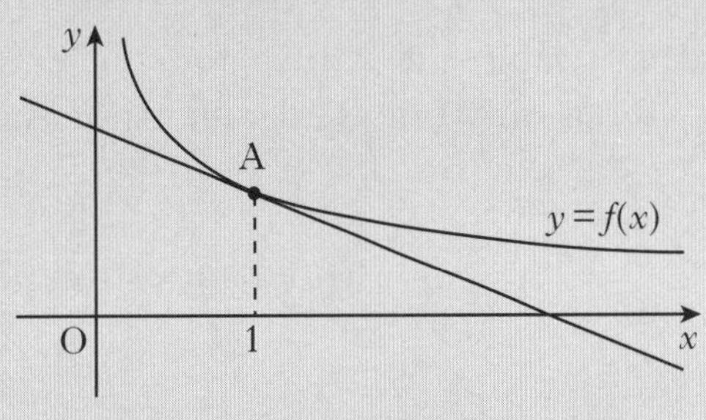

Marks

6. 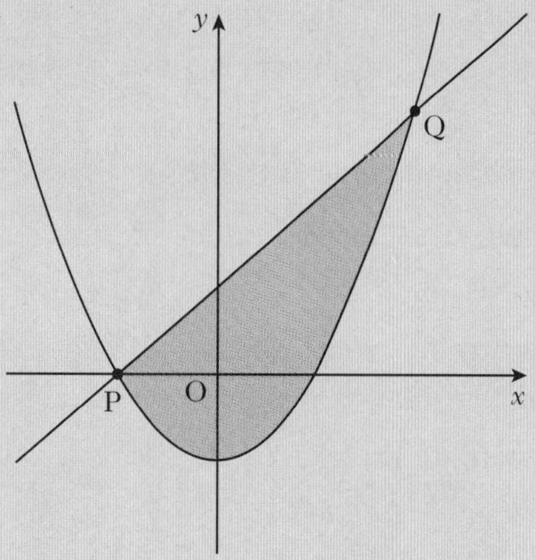

The line with equation $y = x + 1$ intersects the parabola $y = x^2 - 1$ at points P and Q as shown in the diagram.

Calculate the shaded area enclosed by the line and the parabola. **8**

7. The formula $P = 6e^{0{\cdot}0138t}$ is used to predict the population P of the world, in billions, t years after January 1, 2000.

(*a*) What was the population of the world on January 1, 2000? **1**

(*b*) At the start of which year will the world's population be more than double that of the population on January 1, 2000? **4**

8. The diagram shows the graphs of two functions f and g defined by:

$f(x) = a\sin x$

$g(x) = \cos bx$

In the interval $0 \leq x \leq 2\pi$ the two graphs intersect at the three points A, B and C as shown.

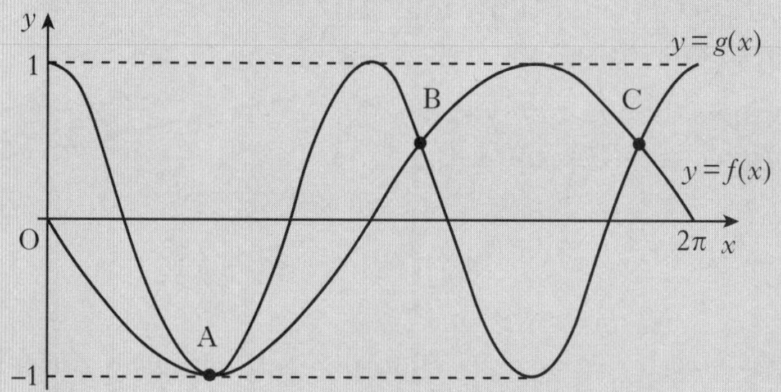

(*a*) Write down the values of a and b. **1**

(*b*) Show algebraically, by solving the equation $f(x) = g(x)$, that at point A $\sin x = 1$. **4**

9. A function f is defined by $f(x) = x^3 + (2 - a)x^2 - ax + 2a$ where x is a Real number and a is a constant.

(*a*) Show that $f(-2) = 0$. **1**

(*b*) Find the range of values for the constant a for which the equation $f(x) = 0$ has only one Real root, namely $x = -2$. **7**

[End of question paper]

Worked Answers

Q1

$3x + 2y - 1 = 0$

$\Rightarrow 2y = -3x + 1$

$\Rightarrow y = -\frac{3}{2}x + \frac{1}{2}$

$\Rightarrow m = -\frac{3}{2}$

Choice B.

2 marks

- Rearrange the equation into the form: $y = mx + c$.
- Steps are:
  1. Subtract $3x$ from both sides of the equation.
  2. Add 1 to both sides of the equation.
  3. Divide both sides of the equation by 2.
- m is the gradient, and lines which are parallel have the same gradient. The gradient of the line with equation $3x + 2y - 1 = 0$ is $-\frac{3}{2}$.

HMRN: p. 4–5

Q2

$2x^2 - 4x + 1$

$= 2\left(x^2 - 2x + \frac{1}{2}\right)$

$= 2\left[(x-1)(x-1) - 1 + \frac{1}{2}\right]$

$= 2\left[(x-1)^2 - \frac{1}{2}\right]$

$= 2(x-1)^2 - 1$

compare $2(x + a)^2 + b$

$\Rightarrow b = -1$

Choice A.

2 marks

- You have to "complete the square".
- The coefficient of x^2 is a difficulty – that is why 2 is removed outside the brackets.
- Notice when $(x - 1)(x - 1)$ is multiplied out you get $x^2 - 2x + 1$. Removing the '+1' allows line 3 to equal line 2 in the working.
- Be careful to include the negative for the value of b: -1 is $+ (-1)$.
- An alternative is:

$2x^2 - 4x + 1 = 2(x^2 - 2x) + 1$

$= 2[(x - 1)(x - 1) - 1] + 1$

$= 2[(x - 1)^2 - 1] + 1 = 2(x - 1)^2 - 2 + 1$

$= 2(x - 1)^2 - 1$

HMRN: p. 13

Q3

Let the limit be L

Then $L = -0{\cdot}2L + 5$

$\Rightarrow L + 0{\cdot}2L = 5$

$\Rightarrow 1{\cdot}2L = 5$

$\Rightarrow L = \frac{5}{1{\cdot}2} = \frac{50}{12} = \frac{25}{6}$

Choice B.

2 marks

- There is a formula that says $L = \frac{b}{1-a}$ for the recurrence relation

$u_{n+1} = au_n + b$. This formula is not given to you in the exam. It is easier to use 'algebra' knowing that L going 'in' to the recurrence relation, i.e. $aL + b$, means L comes 'out', i.e. $L = aL + b$, then solve for L. This approach is taken in the given solution.

HMRN: p. 24

Q4

$$3x^2 - x + c = 0$$

compare $ax^2 + bx + c = 0$

$\Rightarrow a = 3$ and $b = -1$

Discriminant $= b^2 - 4ac$

$= (-1)^2 - 4 \times 3 \times c$

$= 1 - 12c$

For equal roots :

Discriminant $= 0$

So $1 - 12c = 0$

$\Rightarrow 12c = 1 \Rightarrow c = \frac{1}{12}$

Choice C.

2 marks

- For the equation $ax^2 + bx + c = 0$ the two roots are:

$$x = \frac{-b + \sqrt{b^2 - 4ac}}{2a} \quad \text{or} \quad x = \frac{-b - \sqrt{b^2 - 4ac}}{2a}$$

They differ in the numerator by the adding or subtracting of the term $\sqrt{b^2 - 4ac}$. If this term is zero then the two roots are the same, so if $b^2 - 4ac = 0$ the roots are equal.

- $b^2 - 4ac$ is called the Discriminant.
- Remember that squaring a negative number gives a positive answer. $(-1)^2$ is positive 1.

HMRN: p. 28

Q5

$$2\boldsymbol{a} - 3\boldsymbol{b} = \begin{pmatrix} -8 \\ -1 \\ 3 \end{pmatrix}$$

$$\Rightarrow 2\boldsymbol{a} = 3\boldsymbol{b} + \begin{pmatrix} -8 \\ -1 \\ 3 \end{pmatrix}$$

$$\Rightarrow 2\boldsymbol{a} = 3\begin{pmatrix} 2 \\ 1 \\ 5 \end{pmatrix} + \begin{pmatrix} -8 \\ -1 \\ 3 \end{pmatrix}$$

$$\Rightarrow 2\boldsymbol{a} = \begin{pmatrix} 6 \\ 3 \\ 15 \end{pmatrix} + \begin{pmatrix} -8 \\ -1 \\ 3 \end{pmatrix}$$

$$\Rightarrow 2\boldsymbol{a} = \begin{pmatrix} -2 \\ 2 \\ 18 \end{pmatrix}$$

$$\Rightarrow \boldsymbol{a} = \begin{pmatrix} -1 \\ 1 \\ 9 \end{pmatrix}$$

Choice A.

2 marks

- There are two ways of specifying a vector. One is using the unit vectors $\boldsymbol{i}$, $\boldsymbol{j}$ and $\boldsymbol{k}$, e.g. $-\boldsymbol{i} + \boldsymbol{j} + 9\boldsymbol{k}$. The other is the component form: $\begin{pmatrix} -1 \\ 1 \\ 9 \end{pmatrix}$
- The steps in the solution are:
  1. Add $3\boldsymbol{b}$ to both sides of the equation.
  2. Replace $\boldsymbol{b}$ by $\begin{pmatrix} 2 \\ 1 \\ 5 \end{pmatrix}$
  3. Multiply each component of $\boldsymbol{b}$ by 3 to get $3\boldsymbol{b}$ i.e $\begin{pmatrix} 3 \times 2 \\ 3 \times 1 \\ 3 \times 5 \end{pmatrix} = \begin{pmatrix} 6 \\ 3 \\ 15 \end{pmatrix}$
  4. Add the corresponding components: $\begin{pmatrix} 6 \\ 3 \\ 15 \end{pmatrix} + \begin{pmatrix} -8 \\ -1 \\ 3 \end{pmatrix} = \begin{pmatrix} 6 + (-8) \\ 3 + (-1) \\ 15 + 3 \end{pmatrix} = \begin{pmatrix} -2 \\ 2 \\ 18 \end{pmatrix}$
  5. Divide each component by 2 to change $2\boldsymbol{a}$ to $\boldsymbol{a}$.

HMRN: p. 43–44

Q6

$u_0 = \frac{1}{3}$

So $u_1 = 3u_0 - 1$

$= 3 \times \frac{1}{3} - 1 = 1 - 1 = 0$

and $u_2 = 3u_1 - 1 = 3 \times 0 - 1$

$= 0 - 1 = -1$

Choice B.

2 marks

- A helpful diagram is:

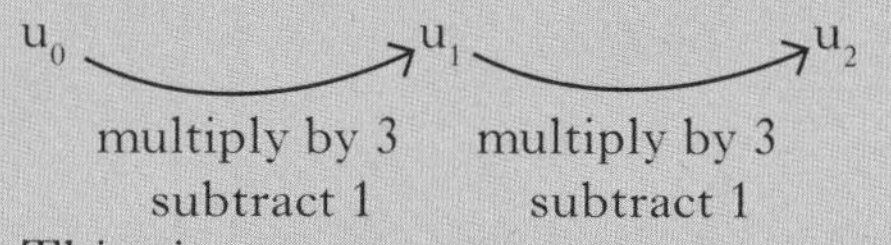

This gives:

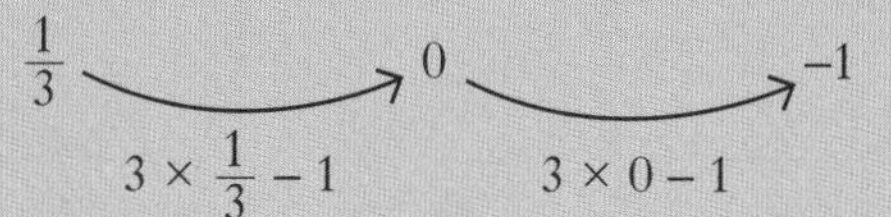

HMRN: p. 23

Q7

There are two cycles in the interval $0 \leq x \leq 2\pi$ so $a = 2$

The sine curve has been moved down 1 unit parallel to the y-axis so $b = -1$

Choice C.

2 marks

- $y = k \sin ax + b$

  k gives the amplitude. In this case 2.

  a gives the number of cycles from 0 to 2π. In this case 2.

  b gives the vertical shift. In this case -1.

- In this type of question the scale on the axis is very important. In this case there is one cycle of a sine curve starting at $x = 0$ and finishing at $x = \pi$.
- The curve $y = 2\sin 2x$ would have a max of 2 and a min of -2. Subtracting 1 from these values gives 1 and -3 as shown in the diagram on the y-axis.

HMRN: p. 16–17

Q8

$$\int \sin 2x + 2x^{-2}\,dx$$

$$= -\frac{\cos 2x}{2} + \frac{2x^{-1}}{-1} + C$$

$$= -\frac{1}{2}\cos 2x - 2x^{-1} + C$$

Choice A.

2 marks

- The rules used are:

  $\int \sin ax\,dx = -\frac{1}{a}\cos ax + C$

  and $\int ax^n\,dx = \frac{ax^{n+1}}{n+1} + C$

  The first of these rules is given to you on your formulae sheet in the exam. The second rule is not. As always you should memorise all formulae so that they are very familiar to you.

- Notice that $\frac{\cos 2x}{2}$ and $\frac{1}{2}\cos 2x$ are identical expressions, as are $\frac{a}{2}$ and $\frac{1}{2}a$.

HMRN: p. 31, p. 49

Q9

$$h\left(g\left(\frac{\pi}{12}\right)\right)$$

$$= h\left(3 \times \frac{\pi}{12}\right)$$

$$= h\left(\frac{\pi}{4}\right)$$

$$= \sin\left(2 \times \frac{\pi}{4}\right)$$

$$= \sin\frac{\pi}{2} = 1$$

Choice B.

2 marks

- Work from the inside out. So deal with $g\left(\frac{\pi}{12}\right)$ first.
- $g(x) = 3x$ so $g\left(\frac{\pi}{12}\right) = 3 \times \frac{\pi}{12} = \frac{3\pi}{12}$ and then cancel by 3.
- $h(x) = \sin 2x$ so $h\left(\frac{\pi}{4}\right) = \sin\left(2 \times \frac{\pi}{4}\right)$

  $= \sin\frac{2\pi}{4}$ and then cancel by 2.

- $\sin\frac{\pi}{2}$ can be obtained by thinking of the graph $y = \sin x$:

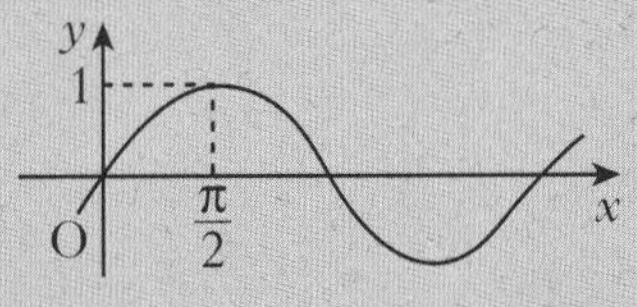

HMRN: p. 10, p. 15

Q10

$x^2 + y^2 + 2x + 4y - 4 = 0$

Centre is $(-1, -2)$

Radius $= \sqrt{(-1)^2 + (-2)^2 - (-4)}$

$= \sqrt{1 + 4 + 4} = \sqrt{9} = 3$

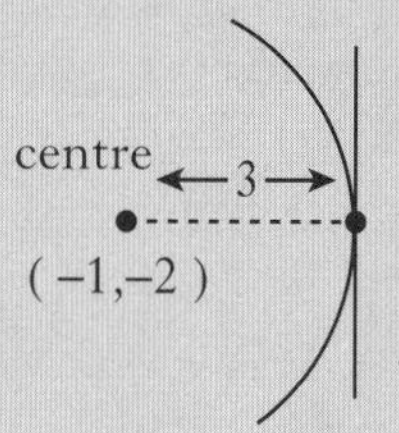

Line L is 3 units to the right of $x = -1$ so the equation is $x = 2$.

Choice C.

2 marks

- All lines parallel to the y-axis have equations of the form $x = k$ for some constant k.
- Since the tangent and the radius to the point of contact are perpendicular, you know that the radius will be parallel to the x-axis:

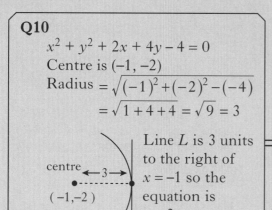

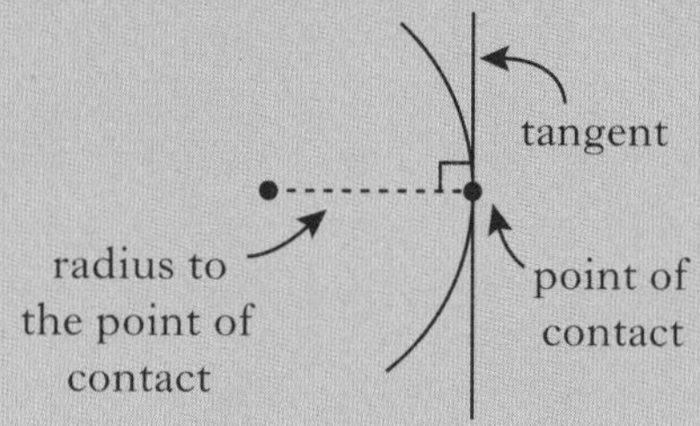

- To then find the centre:

$$x^2 + y^2 + 2gx + 2fy + c = 0$$

$$(-g, -f)$$

Halve the x and y coefficients and then change their signs. In this case the coefficients are 2 and 4. Dividing by 2 gives 1 and 2 then changing sign produces −1 and −2 to give $(-1, -2)$ as the centre.

HMRN: p. 5, p. 39

Q11

The equation of the x-axis is $y = 0$. So solving

$$\left.\begin{aligned} y &= ax^2 + bx + c \\ y &= 0 \end{aligned}\right\}$$

will give one solution as the x-axis is a tangent to the curve. So $ax^2 + bx + c = 0$ has one solution.

i.e. Discriminant = 0

i.e. $b^2 - 4ac = 0$

$\Rightarrow b^2 = 4ac$

Choice D.

2 marks

- To find the points of intersection of a curve $y = f(x)$ with the x-axis you have to set $y = 0$. You therefore get $0 = f(x)$ or $f(x) = 0$, an equation which you solve to produce the values of the x-intercepts.
- The nature of the roots of the equation

$$ax^2 + bx + c = 0$$

are given by:

$b^2 - 4ac > 0$: two Real distinct roots

$b^2 - 4ac = 0$: equal roots

$b^2 - 4ac < 0$: no Real roots.

- Add $4ac$ to both sides of the equation $b^2 - 4ac = 0$ to get $b^2 = 4ac$.

HMRN: p. 28

Q12

Since the vectors are perpendicular:

$$\begin{pmatrix}-1\\k\\3\end{pmatrix}\cdot\begin{pmatrix}-4\\2\\-1\end{pmatrix}=0$$

$\Rightarrow -1\times(-4)+k\times 2+3\times(-1)=0$

$\Rightarrow 4+2k-3=0$

$\Rightarrow 2k+1=0$

$\Rightarrow 2k=-1$

$\Rightarrow k=-\frac{1}{2}$

Choice D.

2 marks

- If two vectors $\boldsymbol{v}$ and $\boldsymbol{w}$ are perpendicular then $\boldsymbol{v}\,.\,\boldsymbol{w}=0$. This is since $\boldsymbol{v}\,.\,\boldsymbol{w}=|\boldsymbol{v}||\boldsymbol{w}|\cos\theta$ where θ is the angle between the two vectors. $\theta=\frac{\pi}{2}$ for perpendicular vectors and $\cos\frac{\pi}{2}=0$ so $\boldsymbol{v}\,.\,\boldsymbol{w}=0$
- $\begin{pmatrix}a_1\\a_2\\a_3\end{pmatrix}\cdot\begin{pmatrix}b_1\\b_2\\b_3\end{pmatrix}=a_1b_1+a_2b_2+a_3b_3$

  This result is given on your formulae sheet in the exam.

HMRN: p. 46

Q13

Let $f(x)=\dfrac{1}{2\sqrt[3]{x}}=\dfrac{1}{2x^{\frac{1}{3}}}=\dfrac{x^{-\frac{1}{3}}}{2}$

$=\frac{1}{2}x^{-\frac{1}{3}}$

so $f'(x)=-\frac{1}{3}\times\frac{1}{2}x^{-\frac{1}{3}-1}$

$=-\frac{1}{6}x^{-\frac{4}{3}}$

Choice A.

2 marks

- The 'derivative' is what you get when you differentiate an expression.
- A common mistake is to move the 2 to the top of the fraction. Think like this: $\dfrac{1}{2x^{\frac{1}{3}}}=\dfrac{1}{2}\times\dfrac{1}{x^{\frac{1}{3}}}=\dfrac{1}{2}\times x^{-\frac{1}{3}}=\dfrac{1}{2}x^{-\frac{1}{3}}$
- The rule used for differentiating is: $f(x)=ax^n\Rightarrow f'(x)=anx^{n-1}$
- Multiplying fractions: $\frac{1}{3}\times\frac{1}{2}=\frac{1\times1}{3\times2}=\frac{1}{6}$
- For the index: $-\frac{1}{3}-1=-\frac{1}{3}-\frac{3}{3}=\frac{-1-3}{3}$ giving $\frac{-4}{3}$ or $-\frac{4}{3}$

HMRN: p. 18–19

Q14

$f'(-1)=0$ means that for $x=-1$ the gradient on the curve is 0 i.e. there is a stationary point – this eliminates Choice A.
$f(1)<0$ means that for $x=1$ the curve lies below the x-axis.
Of the remaining choices this is true of only Choice B.

Choice B.

2 marks

- Remember that $f'(x)$ concerns the gradient on the curve, i.e. the slope, whereas $f(x)$ concerns the height of the graph above (or below) the x-axis.

  So if $f'(x)$ is positive the graph slopes up. If $f'(x)$ is negative the graph slopes down. If $f'(x)$ is zero the graph has a stationary point.

  If $f(x)$ is positive the graph lies above the x-axis. If $f(x)$ is negative the graph lies below the x-axis.

HMRN: p. 19–20

Q15

$V(r) = \frac{4}{3}\pi r^3$

$\Rightarrow V'(r) = 3 \times \frac{4}{3}\pi r^2$

$= 4\pi r^2$

So $V'(1) = 4 \times \pi \times 1^2$

$= 4\pi$

Choice B.

2 marks

- The expression 'rate of change' indicates that you are expected to differentiate.
- There are two difficulties: the letters are not the usual x and y and also π appears in the expression. To help your thinking, let's change to x and y. So $V(r) = \frac{4}{3}\pi r^3$ becomes $f(x) = \frac{4}{3}\pi x^3$ or $y = \frac{4}{3}\pi x^3$. Now think of $\frac{4}{3}\pi$ as just an unknown constant, k say. So finally you have $y = kx^3$. Differentiate giving $\frac{dy}{dx} = 3kx^2$ or $f'(x) = 3kx^2$. Changing back gives $V'(r) = 3 \times \frac{4}{3}\pi r^2 = 4\pi r^2$.
- $V'(1)$ means replace r by the value 1 in the formula $4\pi r^2$, i.e. $4\pi \times 1^2 = 4\pi$.

HMRN: p. 22

Q16

$\int_0^7 g(x)\,dx - \int_0^7 f(x)\,dx$ gives the shaded area so (1) is not correct as the 5 should be 7. (2) is more complicated:

$\int_0^{10} g(x)\,dx$ gives 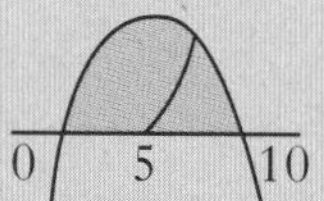

and $-\int_0^5 f(x)\,dx$ gives 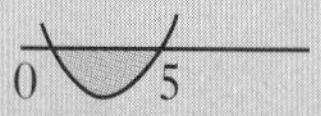

so you need to remove: 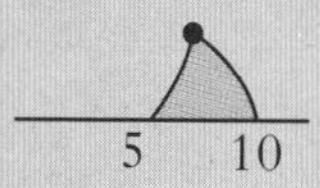

This is not given by $\int_0^{10} f(x)\,dx$ which is:

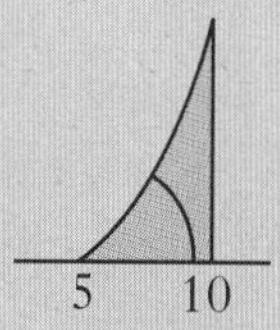

Neither statement is correct so: Choice A.

2 marks

- The main result here is concerned with finding the area between two curves using integration.

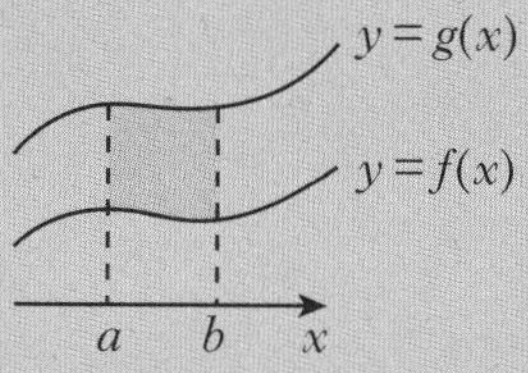

Shaded area $= \int_a^b (g(x) - f(x))\,dx$

$= \int_a^b g(x) - \int_a^b f(x)\,dx$

↑ top curve ↑ bottom curve

- An area below the x-axis will have a negative sign attached:

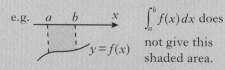

e.g. 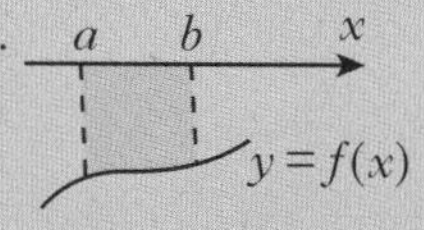

$\int_a^b f(x)\,dx$ does not give this shaded area.

$-\int_a^b f(x)\,dx$ does give this shaded area. The negative sign is necessary since the area lies entirely below the x-axis.

HMRN: p. 32–33

Q17

Find the three x-axis intercepts by solving

$m(x + n)(x + 1)(x + 2) = 0$

$\Rightarrow x + n = 0$ or $x + 1 = 0$ or $x + 2 = 0$

$\Rightarrow x = -n$ or $x = -1$ or $x = -2$

The missing intercept is $x = 2$

So $-n = 2 \Rightarrow n = -2$

Thus $y = m(x - 2)(x + 1)(x + 2)$

The curve passes through $(0, -16)$

So $-16 = m(0 - 2)(0 + 1)(0 + 2)$

$\Rightarrow -16 = m \times (-2) \times 1 \times 2$

$\Rightarrow -16 = m \times (-4)$

$\Rightarrow m = \frac{-16}{-4} = 4$

Choice C.

2 marks

- You have to match features on the given graph to features of the equation. On the graph there are three x-intercepts shown. x-intercepts are determined by setting $y = 0$ and solving the resulting equation: $m(x + n)(x + 1)(x + 2) = 0$. Each 'linear' factor corresponds to one of the x-intercepts:

  $(x + 1)$ corresponds to $x = -1$

  $(x + 2)$ corresponds to $x = -2$.

  This leaves $x = 2$ unaccounted for, so: $(x + n)$ corresponds to $x = 2$.

  Notice that the value of x is the value that makes the factor zero. So in this last case $n = -2$ would give a zero value for the factor $x + n$ when $x = 2$.

- The constant factor m is a y-axis (or vertical) scaling factor which determines the height above or below the x-axis of points on the curve. $(0, -16)$ is the only indication of height on the graph and hence will determine the value of m.

HMRN: p. 26

Q18

$y = \log_b(x + a)$

passes through $(-1, 0)$ so

$y = 0$ when $x = -1$

This gives: $0 = \log_b(-1 + a)$

$\Rightarrow b^0 = -1 + a \Rightarrow 1 = -1 + a$

So $a = 2$

Also $y = \log_b(x + 2)$ passes through $(3, 1)$ so $y = 1$ when $x = 3$

giving : $1 = \log_b(3 + 2)$

$\Rightarrow 1 = \log_b 5$

$\Rightarrow b^1 = 5$, i.e. $b = 5$

equation is $y = \log_5(x + 2)$

Choice D.

2 marks

- Comparing the graph $y = \log_b(x + a)$ with the graph $y = \log_b x$, the value a determines the x-axis (or horizontal) shift. Normally $y = \log_b(x)$ crosses the x-axis of $(1, 0)$. In this example the x-intercept is at $(-1, 0)$. This is a shift of 2 units to the left giving $a = 2$ ($a = -2$ would give a shift to the right of 2 units)

- Results used in this solution are:

  $a = \log_b c \Leftrightarrow b^a = c$

  (log form) (exponential form)

  also $b^0 = 1$ and $b^1 = b$

- Note that if a point lies on a graph then the values of its coordinates must satisfy the equation of the graph.

HMRN: p. 13, p. 50

Q19

Instead of $2x^2 + 5x - 3 < 0$

consider $2x^2 + 5x - 3 = 0$

$\Rightarrow (2x - 1)(x + 3) = 0$

$\Rightarrow 2x - 1 = 0$ or $x + 3 = 0$

$\Rightarrow x = \frac{1}{2}$ or $x = -3$

The graph of $y = 2x^2 + 5x - 3$ is therefore:

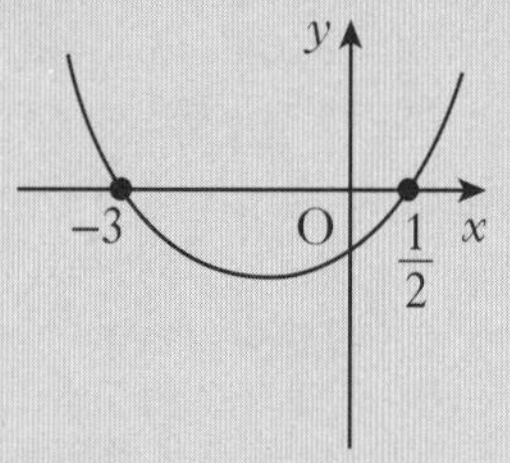

So $2x^2 + 5x - 3 < 0$

for $-3 < x < \frac{1}{2}$

Choice A.

2 marks

- Since this question concerns the values of $2x^2 + 5x - 3$ it makes sense to plot these values, i.e. to investigate the graph $y = 2x^2 + 5x - 3$. This graph is a parabola as shown in the solution opposite.

  The parts of the graph above the x-axis correspond to the values of x for which $2x^2 + 5x - 3 > 0$. Similarly the parts of the graph below the x-axis correspond to the values of x for which $2x^2 + 5x - 3 < 0$. It is this latter part of the graph you are interested in. In this case the corresponding values of x lie between -3 and $\frac{1}{2}$ as shown.
- Having factorised to get $(2x - 1)(x + 3)$ you should always check that the factorisation is correct by multiplying the brackets out. You should get $2x^2 + 5x - 3$.

HMRN: p. 29

Q20

The y-coordinates of all points on the graph $y = 3f\left(\frac{1}{2}x\right)$

are 3 times those on $y = f\left(\frac{1}{2}x\right)$

so $(-6, 12)$ on $y = 3f\left(\frac{1}{2}x\right)$ corresponds to $(-6, 4)$ on $y = f\left(\frac{1}{2}x\right)$.

The minimum $(-6, 4)$ on $y = f\left(\frac{1}{2}x\right)$ occurs when $x = -6$.

This gives $y = f\left(\frac{1}{2} \times (-6)\right) = f(-3)$ and so the corresponding minimum on $y = f(x)$ occurs when $x = -3$ and so is $(-3, 4)$.

Choice B.

2 marks

- The y-coordinate 12 is 3 times the y-coordinate 4.
- One way of understanding this question better is by choosing a particular function that you are familiar with. For example $f(x) = \sin x$. Here are the corresponding expressions and graphs:

$y = f(x)$

$y = \sin(x)$

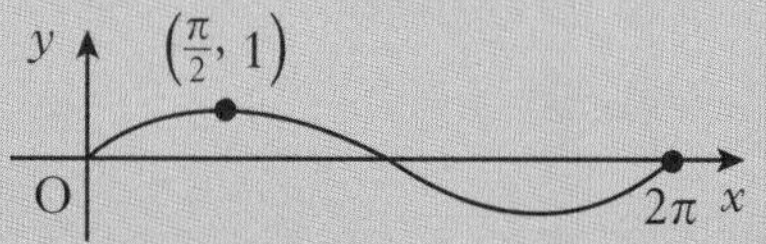

$y = f\left(\frac{1}{2}x\right)$

$y = \sin\frac{1}{2}x$

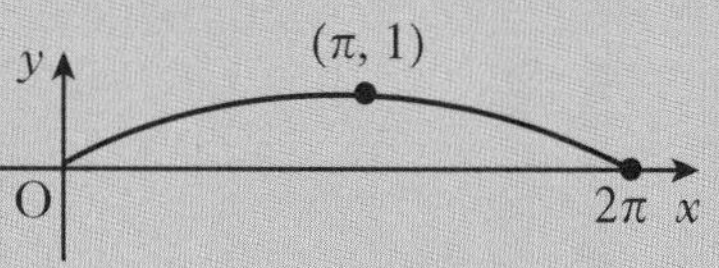

$y = 3f\left(\frac{1}{2}x\right)$

$y = 3\sin\frac{1}{2}x$

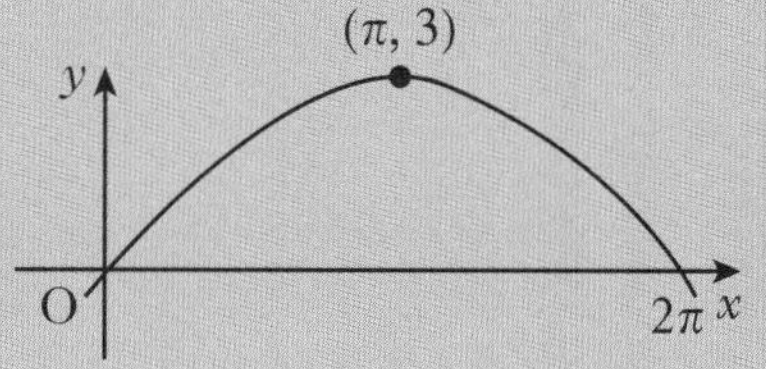

Using the maximum $(\pi, 3)$ on $y = 3f\left(\frac{1}{2}x\right)$, this becomes $(\pi, 1)$ on $y = f\left(\frac{1}{2}x\right)$ and then $\left(\frac{\pi}{2}, 1\right)$ on $y = f(x)$. So divide y-coordinate by 3 then halve the x-coordinate.

HMRN: p. 9, p. 16

Q21(*a*)(*i*)

-1	2	3	0	-1
		-2	-1	1
	2	1	-1	0

✓

So since $h(-1) = 0$ ✓

$x + 1$ is a factor of $h(x)$

2 marks

Calculation
- You are using 'synthetic division' with $x = -1$. This corresponds to dividing by $x + 1$. The calculation shows the remainder is zero.

Conclusion
- You must clearly state that the appearance of zero means that $x + 1$ is a factor.

Q21(*a*)(*ii*)

$h(x) = (x + 1)(2x^2 + x - 1)$ ✓

$= (x + 1)(2x - 1)(x + 1)$

$= (x + 1)^2(2x - 1)$ ✓

2 marks

Quadratic factor
- 2 1 −1 are the coefficients of the other factor $2x^2 + x - 1$.

Full factorisation
- $2x^2 + x - 1$ can be factored: $(2x - 1)(x + 1)$. $(x + 1)(2x^2 + x - 1)$ will not gain this 2nd mark.

Q21(*a*)(*iii*)

$h(x) = 0 \Rightarrow (x + 1)^2(2x - 1) = 0$

$\Rightarrow x + 1 = 0$ or $2x - 1 = 0$

$\Rightarrow x = -1$ or $x = \frac{1}{2}$ ✓

1 mark

Solutions
- This mark is for correctly obtaining both solutions. The mark can still be gained from a wrong factorisation in part (*ii*).

HMRN: p. 25–26

Q21(*b*)

The curves intersect where $f(x) = g(x)$ ✓

$\Rightarrow 2x^3 + x - 3 = -3x^2 + x - 2$

$\Rightarrow 2x^3 + x - 3 + 3x^2 - x + 2 = 0$

$\Rightarrow 2x^3 + 3x^2 - 1 = 0$ ✓

$\Rightarrow x = -1$ or $x = \frac{1}{2}$ (from(*a*)) ✓

For a common tangent $f'(x) = g'(x)$ at the point of intersection. ✓

$f(x) = 2x^3 + x - 3$

$\Rightarrow f'(x) = 6x^2 + 1$

$g(x) = -3x^2 + x - 2$

$\Rightarrow g'(x) = -6x + 1$

$f'(-1) = 6 \times (-1)^2 + 1 = 7$

$g'(-1) = -6 \times (-1) + 1 = 7$

$f'\left(\frac{1}{2}\right) = 6 \times \left(\frac{1}{2}\right)^2 + 1 = \frac{5}{2}$

$g'\left(\frac{1}{2}\right) = -6 \times \frac{1}{2} + 1 = -2$ ✓

So only $x = -1$ gives a common tangent.

The y-coordinate of T is given by:

$f(-1) = 2 \times (-1)^3 + (-1) - 3$

$= -2 - 1 - 3 = -6$

So T(−1,−6) ✓

6 marks

Strategy
- A 'common point' implies a point of intersection. Setting the two expressions equal and solving will find the x-coordinates of the points of intersection.

Standard form
- This is a cubic equation. It has already been solved in part (*a*) of the question.

Solutions
- This mark is for recognising the equation from part (*a*) and stating the solutions again.

Strategy
- If the curves share a common tangent at a point of intersection the gradients of the curves at that point must be equal. Which value, −1 or $\frac{1}{2}$, gives the common point of tangency can only be determined by finding the gradients of both curves at these points.

Differentiate and evaluate
- Notice that when $x = \frac{1}{2}$ the gradients on the two curves are different, i.e. $\frac{5}{2}$ and −2, but that when $x = -1$ the gradients are the same, i.e. 7. So a common tangent is only possible at the point where $x = -1$.

Coordinates
- You should also double-check that $g(-1)$ gives the same result: $g(-1) = -3 \times (-1)^2 + (-1) - 2 = -6$.

HMRN: p. 18–20

Q22(*a*)

T is the midpoint of PQ

So $T\left(\frac{-2+6}{2}, \frac{0+2}{2}\right) = T(2, 1)$ ✓

Using R(1, −3) and T(2, 1)

$\Rightarrow m_{RT} = \frac{-3-1}{1-2} = \frac{-4}{-1} = 4$ ✓

A point on RT is (2, 1) and the gradient of RT is 4 so equation of RT is

$y - 1 = 4(x - 2)$

$\Rightarrow y - 1 = 4x - 8$

$\Rightarrow y = 4x - 7$ ✓

3 marks

Strategy

- You should know that a median is a line from a vertex to the midpoint of the opposite side.
- The midpoint of the line joining (x_1, y_1) and (x_2, y_2) is given by $\left(\frac{x_1+x_2}{2}, \frac{y_1+y_2}{2}\right)$. You should learn this formula as it is not given to you in the exam.

Gradient

- The gradient of the line joining $A(x_1, y_1)$ and $B(x_2, y_2)$ is given by:

$m_{AB} = \frac{y_2 - y_1}{x_2 - x_1} \quad (x_1 \neq x_2)$

- Notice the order can be changed on top *and* bottom of fraction:

$\frac{1-(-3)}{2-1} = \frac{1+3}{1} = \frac{4}{1} = 4$

Equation

- The line passing through (a, b) with gradient m is given by $y - b = m(x - a)$.

HMRN: p. 6–7

Q22(*b*)

The x-intercept is given by setting $y = 0$

$\Rightarrow 4x - 7 = 0$

$\Rightarrow 4x = 7$

$\Rightarrow x = \frac{7}{4}$

So $S\left(\frac{7}{4}, 0\right)$ ✓

1 mark

Coordinates

- x-axis intercepts are given by setting $y = 0$ in the equation of RT.
- You are asked for the coordinates of a point so $x = \frac{7}{4}$ would not gain the mark. The coordinates of a point are needed, i.e. $\left(\frac{7}{4}, 0\right)$.

HMRN: p. 6

Q22(*c*)

$R(1, -3)$, $S\left(\frac{7}{4}, 0\right)$, $T(2, 1)$

$\overrightarrow{RS} = \boldsymbol{s} - \boldsymbol{r} = \begin{pmatrix} 7/4 \\ 0 \end{pmatrix} - \begin{pmatrix} 1 \\ -3 \end{pmatrix} = \begin{pmatrix} 3/4 \\ 3 \end{pmatrix}$

and $\overrightarrow{ST} = \boldsymbol{t} - \boldsymbol{s} = \begin{pmatrix} 2 \\ 1 \end{pmatrix} - \begin{pmatrix} 7/4 \\ 0 \end{pmatrix} = \begin{pmatrix} 1/4 \\ 1 \end{pmatrix}$

$\Rightarrow \overrightarrow{RS} = 3\overrightarrow{ST}$ ✓

So S divides RT in the ratio 3:1 ✓

2 marks

Strategy

- A 'vector approach' is given but there are alternative methods. For example a 'stepping out' approach:

Use the x-coordinates

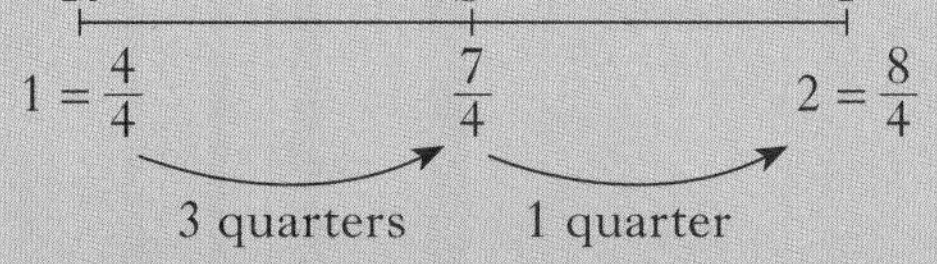

or use the y-coordinates:

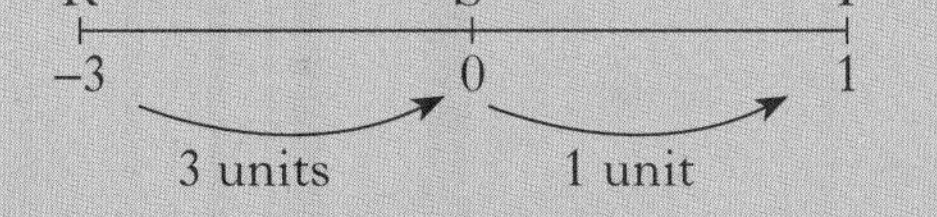

In both cases the ratio 3:1 is indicated.

Ratio

- This 2nd mark is for stating 3:1. Note that 1:3 is wrong as this is the ratio S divides TR not RT. The order is important.

HMRN: p. 45

Q23(a)

$3y - x = 0$

$\Rightarrow 3y = x$

$\Rightarrow y = \frac{1}{3}x$ ✓

So the gradient of line $L = \frac{1}{3}$

So $\tan a° = \frac{1}{3}$ ✓

2 marks

Strategy

- This mark is for knowing to rearrange the line equation into the form $y = mx + c$. In this case $m = \frac{1}{3}$ and $c = 0$.

tan$a$° = gradient

- The result you should know is:

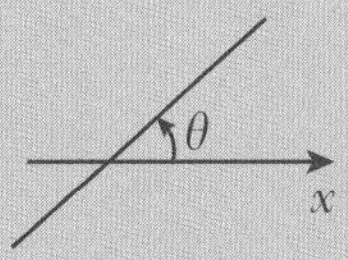

gradient of line $= \tan\theta$

HMRN: p. 4

Q23(b)

$\tan a° = \frac{1}{3}$

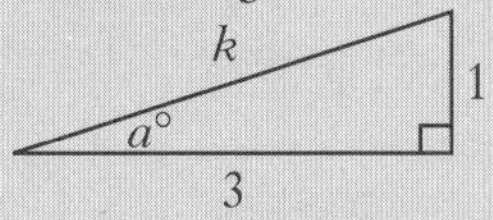

$k^2 = 3^2 + 1^2$

$k^2 = 9 + 1 = 10$

$\Rightarrow k = \sqrt{10}$ ✓

so $\sin a° = \frac{1}{\sqrt{10}}$ ✓

2 marks

Strategy

- If you know the exact value of sin$a$°, cos$a$° or tan$a$° you can construct a right-angled triangle to fit this value and then use Pythagoras' Theorem to find the third side.
- This mark is for drawing the triangle and calculating the hypotenuse.

sin$a$°

- Remember SOHCAHTOA: sine is Opposite divided by Hypotenuse.

Q23(c)

$\sin (a + 45)°$

$= \sin a° \cos 45° + \cos a° \sin 45°$ ✓

$= \frac{1}{\sqrt{10}} \times \frac{1}{\sqrt{2}} + \frac{3}{\sqrt{10}} \times \frac{1}{\sqrt{2}}$ ✓ ✓

$= \frac{1}{\sqrt{20}} + \frac{3}{\sqrt{20}} = \frac{1+3}{\sqrt{20}} = \frac{4}{\sqrt{20}}$ ✓

$= \frac{4}{2\sqrt{5}} = \frac{4 \times \sqrt{5}}{2\sqrt{5} \times \sqrt{5}} = \frac{4\sqrt{5}}{10}$

$= \frac{2\sqrt{5}}{5}$ ✓

5 marks

Addition formula

- This mark is for expanding $\sin(a + 45)°$

sin45° & cos45°

- The exact value of sin45° and cos45° is $\frac{1}{\sqrt{2}}$.

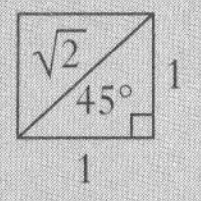

Substitution

- This mark is for replacing sin$a$°, cos$a$°, sin45° and cos45° by $\frac{1}{\sqrt{10}}, \frac{3}{\sqrt{10}}, \frac{1}{\sqrt{2}}$ and $\frac{1}{\sqrt{2}}$ respectively.

Fractions

- Using $\frac{a}{b} \times \frac{c}{d} = \frac{ac}{bd}$ and $\frac{a}{c} + \frac{b}{c} = \frac{a+b}{c}$ to get $\frac{4}{\sqrt{20}}$.

Rationalisation

- Get rid of $\sqrt{5}$ in the denominator showing your working clearly to gain this final mark.

HMRN: p. 35–36

Q23(*d*)

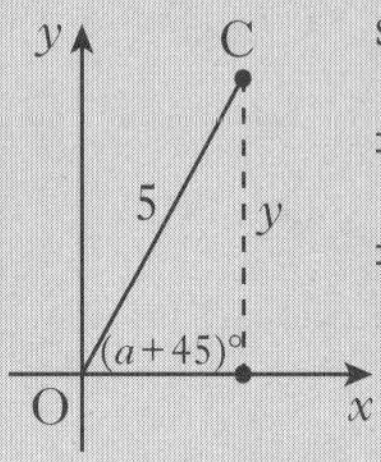

$\sin(a + 45)° = \frac{y}{5}$ ✓

$\Rightarrow \frac{2\sqrt{5}}{5} = \frac{y}{5}$

$\Rightarrow 2\sqrt{5} = y$

So the y-coordinate of point C is $2\sqrt{5}$ ✓

2 marks

Strategy

- This mark is gained for realising that you need to use $\sin(a + 45)°$ in a new triangle with OC as hypotenuse. Usually in questions with several parts, (*a*), (*b*), (*c*) etc, previous answers are used to find later answers.

***y*-coordinate**

- The value $\sin(a + 45)° = \frac{2\sqrt{5}}{5}$ from part (*c*) is used to create an equation in y.
- Multiply both sides by 5 to get rid of fractions.

Q23(*e*)

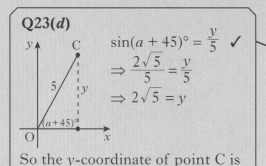

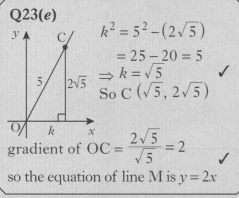

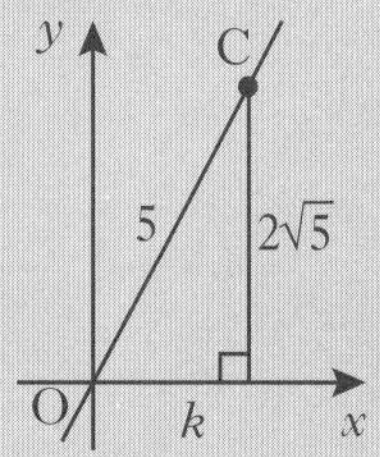

$k^2 = 5^2 - (2\sqrt{5})$

$= 25 - 20 = 5$

$\Rightarrow k = \sqrt{5}$ ✓

So C $(\sqrt{5}, 2\sqrt{5})$

gradient of OC $= \frac{2\sqrt{5}}{\sqrt{5}} = 2$ ✓

so the equation of line M is $y = 2x$

2 marks

Strategy

- The gradient of OC is the y-coordinate of point C divided by its x-coordinate, this is the tan of the angle OC makes with the x-axis.
- Pythagoras' Theorem is used to find the third side of the triangle.

Equation

- Since the line passes through the origin it has equation of the form $y = mx$.

HMRN: p. 5

Q1(*a*)

$2\sin x° - \cos x° = k\sin(x - a)°$
$= k\sin x°\cos a° - k\cos x°\sin a°$ ✓

$\Rightarrow k\cos a° = 2$, $k\sin a° = 1$ } Since $\sin a° > 0$ and $\cos a° > 0$, $a°$ is in the 1st quadrant. ✓

Divide: $\dfrac{k\sin a°}{k\cos a°} = \dfrac{1}{2}$

$\Rightarrow \tan a° = \dfrac{1}{2}$

$\Rightarrow a \doteqdot 26{\cdot}6$ ✓

Square and add:

$(k\sin a°)^2 + (k\cos a°)^2 = 1^2 + 2^2$
$\Rightarrow k^2\sin^2 a° + k^2\cos^2 a° = 1 + 4$
$\Rightarrow k^2(\sin^2 a° + \cos^2 a°) = 5$
$\Rightarrow k^2 \times 1 = 5$
$\Rightarrow k = \sqrt{5}\ (k > 0)$ ✓

So $2\sin x° - \cos x°$
$= \sqrt{5}\sin(x - 26{\cdot}6)°$
(to 1 decimal place).

4 marks

Addition formula

- For the correct expansion of $k\sin(x - a)°$ you will gain this first mark.
- Your formulae sheet has:

  $\sin(A \pm B) = \sin A\cos B \pm \cos A\sin B$
- Notice that the constant k multiplies both terms in the expansion.

Equations

- This mark is for $k\cos a° = 2$ and $k\sin a° = 1$
- The usual method is to compare the coefficients of first $\sin x°$, namely 2 on the left of the equation and $k\cos a°$ on the right giving $k\cos a° = 2$. The corresponding coefficients of $\cos x°$ are -1 and $-k\sin a°$.
- An alternative method:
  Substitute $x = 0$
  $2\sin 0° - \cos 0° =$
  $k\sin 0°\cos a° - k\cos 0°\sin a°$
  $\Rightarrow 0 - 1 = 0 - k \times 1 \times \sin a°$
  $\Rightarrow -1 = -k\sin a° \Rightarrow k\sin a° = 1$
  Substitute $x = 90$
  $2\sin 90° - \cos 90°$
  $= k\sin 90°\cos a° - k\cos 90°\sin a°$
  $\Rightarrow 2 \times 1 - 0 = k \times 1 \times \cos a° - 0$
  $\Rightarrow 2 = k\cos a° \Rightarrow k\cos a° = 2$

Value of *a*

- You are dividing the left-hand and right-hand sides of the equations $k\sin a° = 1$ and $k\cos a° = 2$ and using $\dfrac{\sin a°}{\cos a°} = \tan a°$.

HMRN: p. 53–54

Value of *k*

- This mark is for obtaining $k = \sqrt{5}$
- You are squaring and adding the left-hand and right-hand sides of the two equations:

  $k\sin a° = 1$ and $k\cos a° = 2$

Q1(*b*)

$2\sin x^\circ - \cos x^\circ = \frac{\sqrt{5}}{2}$

$\Rightarrow \sqrt{5}\sin(x - 26{\cdot}6)^\circ = \frac{\sqrt{5}}{2}$ ✓

$\Rightarrow \sin(x - 26{\cdot}6)^\circ = \frac{1}{2}$ ✓

Now $\sin(x - 26{\cdot}6)^\circ$ is positive when $(x - 26{\cdot}6)^\circ$ is in 1st or 2nd quadrants

$\Rightarrow x - 26{\cdot}6\ldots = 30$ or $x - 26{\cdot}6\ldots = 180 - 30$

$\Rightarrow x = 30 + 26{\cdot}6\ldots$ or $x = 150 + 26{\cdot}6\ldots$ ✓

$\Rightarrow x = 56{\cdot}6\ldots$ or $x = 176{\cdot}6\ldots$ ✓

$\Rightarrow x \doteqdot 56{\cdot}6$ or $x \doteqdot 176{\cdot}6$ (to 1 decimal place)

4 marks

Use previous result
- $2\sin x^\circ - \cos x^\circ = \sqrt{5}\sin(x - 26{\cdot}6)^\circ$ from part (*a*).

Simplification
- Divide both sides of the equation by $\sqrt{5}$ to simplify to the form: sin (angle) = value.

Start the solution
- The 'angle' is $(x - 26{\cdot}6)^\circ$. Normally the equation $\sin\theta^\circ = \frac{1}{2}$ gives $\theta = 30$ or 150 so in this case you have $x - 26{\cdot}6$ taking the values 30 or 150.

Complete the solution
- To obtain the value for x, 26·6 is added to the values 30 and 150.
- Any correct rounding will be accepted.

HMRN: p. 54

Q2(*a*)

A(0, 4, 3) and B(10, 0, 6) ✓ ✓

2 marks

Coordinates of A
- z-coordinate is $\frac{1}{3}$ of 9.

Coordinates of B
- z-coordinate is $\frac{2}{3}$ of 9.

HMRN: p. 42

Q2(*b*)

$\overrightarrow{BA} = \boldsymbol{a} - \boldsymbol{b} = \begin{pmatrix}0\\4\\3\end{pmatrix} - \begin{pmatrix}10\\0\\6\end{pmatrix} = \begin{pmatrix}-10\\4\\-3\end{pmatrix}$ ✓

$\overrightarrow{BP} = \boldsymbol{p} - \boldsymbol{b} = \begin{pmatrix}10\\4\\9\end{pmatrix} - \begin{pmatrix}10\\0\\6\end{pmatrix} = \begin{pmatrix}0\\4\\3\end{pmatrix}$ ✓

2 marks

Components of $\overrightarrow{BA}$
- The important position vector result is used: $\overrightarrow{PQ} = \boldsymbol{q} - \boldsymbol{p}$, $\overrightarrow{ST} = \boldsymbol{t} - \boldsymbol{s}$ etc.

Components of $\overrightarrow{BP}$
- Order is important: $\boldsymbol{p} - \boldsymbol{b}$ not $\boldsymbol{b} - \boldsymbol{p}$.

HMRN: p. 42

Q2(*c*)

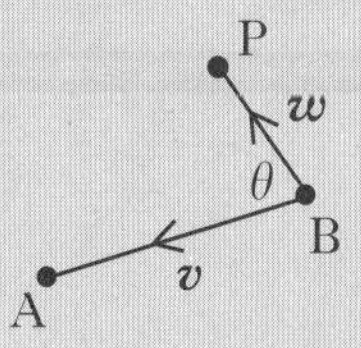

$\cos\theta = \dfrac{\boldsymbol{v}\cdot\boldsymbol{w}}{|\boldsymbol{v}|\,|\boldsymbol{w}|}$ ✓

$\boldsymbol{v}\cdot\boldsymbol{w} = \begin{pmatrix}-10\\4\\-3\end{pmatrix}\cdot\begin{pmatrix}0\\4\\3\end{pmatrix}$ ✓

$= -10\times 0 + 4\times 4 + (-3)\times 3 = 7$

$|\boldsymbol{v}| = \sqrt{(-10)^2 + 4^2 + (-3)^2}$

$= \sqrt{125} = 5\sqrt{5}$

$|\boldsymbol{w}| = \sqrt{0^2 + 4^2 + 3^2} = \sqrt{25} = 5$ ✓

So

$\cos\theta° = \dfrac{7}{5\sqrt{5}\times 5} = \dfrac{7}{25\sqrt{5}} = \dfrac{7\sqrt{5}}{125}$

$\Rightarrow \theta = \cos^{-1}\left(\dfrac{7\sqrt{5}}{125}\right) = 82{\cdot}806\ldots$

angle ABP $\doteqdot 82{\cdot}8°$ ✓
(to 1 decimal place).

4 marks

Scalar Product
- You should know to use:
  $\cos A\hat{B}P = \dfrac{\overrightarrow{BA}\,.\,\overrightarrow{BP}}{|\overrightarrow{BA}|\,|\overrightarrow{BP}|}$
- On your formulae sheet you are given the result:
  $\boldsymbol{a}\,.\,\boldsymbol{b} = |\boldsymbol{a}|\,|\boldsymbol{b}|\cos\theta$

Calculation of Scalar Product
- Your formulae sheet has:

  $\boldsymbol{a}\,.\,\boldsymbol{b} = a_1b_1 + a_2b_2 + a_3b_3$

  where $\boldsymbol{a} = \begin{pmatrix}a_1\\a_2\\a_3\end{pmatrix}$ and $\boldsymbol{b} = \begin{pmatrix}b_1\\b_2\\b_3\end{pmatrix}$

Magnitudes of $\boldsymbol{v}$ and $\boldsymbol{w}$
- The result here is

  $|\boldsymbol{v}| = \sqrt{a^2 + b^2 + c^2}$ where $\boldsymbol{v} = \begin{pmatrix}a\\b\\c\end{pmatrix}$
- Remember, squaring a negative number gives a positive result.
- Take care with numerical calculations.

Angle
- Degree or Radian measure will both gain this mark. Also any correct rounding is acceptable.
- The brackets in $\cos^{-1}(7\sqrt{5}/125)$ are vital when using your calculator.

HMRN: p. 46

Q3

$\Rightarrow 2\cos 2x + 7\sin x = 0$

$\Rightarrow 2(1 - 2\sin^2 x) + 7\sin x = 0$ ✓

$\Rightarrow 2 - 4\sin^2 x + 7\sin x = 0$

$\Rightarrow 4\sin^2 x - 7\sin x - 2 = 0$ ✓

$\Rightarrow (4\sin x + 1)(\sin x - 2) = 0$ ✓

So $\sin x - 2 = 0 \Rightarrow \sin x = 2$
and there are no solutions,

or $4\sin x + 1 = 0 \Rightarrow \sin x = -\frac{1}{4}$ ✓

x is in the 3rd or 4th quadrant.

The 1st quadrant angle is $0{\cdot}2526\ldots$

$\Rightarrow x = \pi + 0{\cdot}2526\ldots = 3{\cdot}394\ldots$
or $x = 2\pi - 0{\cdot}2526\ldots = 6{\cdot}030\ldots$
So the solutions are:
$3{\cdot}39$ or $6{\cdot}03$ ✓
to 3 significant figures.

5 marks

Double angle formula
- To gain this mark there should be evidence that you knew to replace $\cos 2x$ by a suitable equivalent expression.
- Since $\sin x$ appears already in the equation then $1 - 2\sin^2 x$ is suitable, not $2\cos^2 x - 1$.

Quadratic form
- Rearrange to 'standard' quadratic form, i.e. $a\sin^2 x + b\sin x + c = 0$.

Factorisation
- Compare $4s^2 - 7s - 2 = (4s + 1)(s - 2)$.

Values of $\sin x$
- This mark is for the appearance of

  $\sin x = 2$ and $\sin x = -\frac{1}{4}$.

Solutions
- At some point there should be a clear statement following $\sin x = 2$ that this possibility leads to no solutions, otherwise this mark will be lost.
- The equation is in Radian measure. Solutions in degrees will lose this mark.

HMRN: p. 37

Q4

$y = (2 - 3x)^{\frac{4}{3}}$

$\Rightarrow \frac{dy}{dx} = \frac{4}{3}(2 - 3x)^{\frac{1}{3}} \times (-3)$ ✓

$= -4(2 - 3x)^{\frac{1}{3}} = -4\sqrt[3]{2 - 3x}$ ✓

when $x = -2$, $\frac{dy}{dx} = -4\sqrt[3]{2 - 3 \times (-2)}$

$= -4\sqrt[3]{2 + 6} = -4\sqrt[3]{8} = -4 \times 2 = -8$ ✓

Now $y = (2 - 3x)^{\frac{4}{3}} = (\sqrt[3]{2 - 3x})^4$

when $x = -2$

$y = (\sqrt[3]{2 - 3(-2)})^4 = 2^4 = 16$ ✓

A point on the tangent is $(-2, 16)$ and the gradient is -8.

Equation is $y - 16 = -8(x - (-2))$

$\Rightarrow y - 16 = -8(x + 2)$

$\Rightarrow y - 16 = -8x - 16$

$\Rightarrow y = -8x$ ✓

5 marks

Start to differentiate

- Appearance of $\frac{4}{3}(2 - 3x)^{\frac{1}{3}}$ will gain this mark.
- Remember that when you differentiate you are finding a formula for the gradient of the curve.

Chain rule

- The factor -3 results from applying the 'chain rule': $y = (f(x))^n$

$$\Rightarrow \frac{dy}{dx} = n(f(x))^{n-1} \times f'(x)$$

In this case $f(x) = 2 - 3x$ and $n = \frac{4}{3}$.

Gradient

- Recall that $a^{\frac{1}{2}} = \sqrt{a}$, $a^{\frac{1}{3}} = \sqrt[3]{a}$ etc.

***y*-coordinate**

- Use $\frac{dy}{dx}$ for obtaining the gradient, but use y for obtaining the point on the curve, i.e substitute $x = -2$ in $(2 - 3x)^{\frac{4}{3}}$.

Equation

- You are using this result: $y - b = m(x - a)$ is the equation of a line passing through (a, b) with gradient m. In this case (a, b) is $(-2, 16)$ and $m = -8$.

HMRN: p. 20, p. 48–49

Q5(*a*)

For the points of intersection

Solve: $\left.\begin{array}{l} y = 2x^3 \\ y = x^2 \end{array}\right\} \Rightarrow 2x^3 = x^2$

$\Rightarrow 2x^3 - x^2 = 0$

$\Rightarrow x^2(2x - 1) = 0$

$\Rightarrow x = 0$ or $2x - 1 = 0$

$x = 0$ gives the origin

$2x - 1 = 0 \Rightarrow x = \frac{1}{2}$

so the x-coordinate of point P is $\frac{1}{2}$ ✓

1 mark

***x*-coordinate**

- An alternative way to solve this equation is to divide both sides by x^2:

$$2x^3 = x^2 \Rightarrow \frac{2x^3}{x^2} = \frac{x^2}{x^2} \Rightarrow 2x = 1 \Rightarrow x = \frac{1}{2}$$

However there is a danger. What if $x = 0$? Division by zero is not allowed. So providing $x \neq 0$ then $x = \frac{1}{2}$. You need then to let $x = 0$ in the original equation and you find that $x = 0$ is a possible solution (in this case giving the origin as a point of intersection).

Q5(*b*)(*i*)

$QR = x^2 - 2x^3 = x^2(1 - 2x)$ ✓

1 mark

Expression

- The 'height' of points on the curve $y = x^2$ is given by the expression x^2. If $x = 3$ for example, 3^2 is the height of the corresponding point above the x-axis, i.e. 9 units. So x^2 and $2x^3$ give the heights of the curves for a particular value of x. So $x^2 - 2x^3$ will give the 'gap' between the curves.
- Factorisation was not essential here.

Q5(*b*)(*ii*)

$QR^2 = [x^2(1 - 2x)]^2$

$= x^4(1 - 2x)^2 = x^4(1 - 4x + 4x^2)$

$= x^4 - 4x^5 + 4x^6$

So $A(x) = 4x^6 - 4x^5 + x^4$ ✓

1 mark

Area expression
- Note that a square of side k units has area k^2 units^2. This is why you need to square the expression from part (i) above.

Q5(*c*)

$A(x) = 4x^6 - 4x^5 + x^4$

$\Rightarrow A'(x) = 24x^5 - 20x^4 + 4x^3$ ✓

For stationary points set $A'(x) = 0$

$\Rightarrow 24x^5 - 20x^4 + 4x^3 = 0$ ✓

$\Rightarrow 4x^3(6x^2 - 5x + 1) = 0$

$\Rightarrow 4x^3(2x - 1)(3x - 1) = 0$ ✓

$\Rightarrow x = 0$ or $2x - 1 = 0$ or $3x - 1 = 0$

$\Rightarrow x = \frac{1}{2}$ $\quad\Rightarrow x = \frac{1}{3}$

The permitted range is $0 < x < \frac{1}{2}$ so $x = 0$ and $x = \frac{1}{2}$ are not valid solutions. ✓

For $x = \frac{1}{3}$

		$\frac{1}{3}$		
$A'(x) = 4x^3(2x-1)(3x-1)$:	+		−	
Shape of graph:	/	−	\	✓

So $x = \frac{1}{3}$ gives a maximum value for $A(x)$.

Since $A(x) = x^4(1 - 2x)^2$

then $A\left(\frac{1}{3}\right) = \left(\frac{1}{3}\right)^4\left(1 - 2 \times \frac{1}{3}\right)$

$= \frac{1}{81}\left(1 - \frac{2}{3}\right)^2 = \frac{1}{81} \times \left(\frac{1}{3}\right)^2 = \frac{1}{81} \times \frac{1}{9}$

$= \frac{1}{729}$ units^2 which is the maximum value. ✓

6 marks

Differentiate
- You should know that to hunt down maximum or minimum values you need to differentiate.

Set derivative to zero
- These max or min points on a graph are the places where the gradient is zero, i.e. $A'(x) = 0$.

Solutions
- The common factor is $4x^3$ and when removed leaves a quadratic factor $6x^2 - 5x + 1$ which can be factored further into two linear factors: $2x - 1$ and $3x - 1$.

Allowed solution
- In many questions like this not all stationary points on the graph are within the allowed range of x-values, in this case only $x = \frac{1}{3}$ is allowed.

Nature
- Having established that there is a stationary point when $x = \frac{1}{3}$ you have to show that it is a maximum stationary point. This mark is for displaying a 'nature table'.
- The working shows the minimum requirement for this table: a row labelled $A'(x)$ showing the sign of the gradient to the left and to the right of $x = \frac{1}{3}$ and a row labelled 'shape of graph' indicating the slope of the graph on either side of the stationary point.
- You must state clearly your interpretation of the nature table, i.e. you have found a maximum value.

Maximum value
- The question specifically asks for the maximum value of the area, so the value $A(\frac{1}{3})$ is required.
- $\frac{1}{729}$ units^2 is the exact value but marks would be gained for a correct decimal approximation, e.g. 0·0014 units^2.

HMRN: p. 20–21

Q6(*a*)

Solve $y = 2x + 7$ and $x^2 + y^2 - 4x - 2y - 15 = 0$

$\Rightarrow x^2 + (2x + 7)^2 - 4x - 2(2x + 7) - 15 = 0$ ✓

$\Rightarrow x^2 + 4x^2 + 28x + 49 - 4x - 4x - 14 - 15 = 0$

$\Rightarrow 5x^2 + 20x + 20 = 0$ ✓

$\Rightarrow 5(x + 2)(x + 2) = 0 \Rightarrow x = -2$ ✓

Since there is only one solution the line is a tangent to the circle. ✓

When $x = -2$,

$y = 2 \times (-2) + 7 = 3$

So the point of contact is

P(−2, 3) ✓

5 marks

Substitution
- You take the circle equation and replace every occurrence of y with $2x + 7$.

Standard form
- Multiply out and simplify. You should recognise a quadratic equation and therefore rearrange into the form $ax^2 + bx + c = 0$.

Solution
- Remember to take out any common factor as this makes quadratic factorising easier.

Statement
- "One solution ⇒ a tangent". This fact must be clearly stated. There are three situations that can arise concerning a line intersecting a circle:

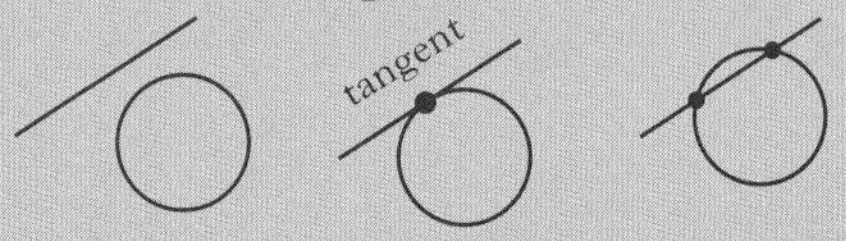

no points of intersection (no solutions) — one point of intersection (one solution) — two points of intersection (two solutions)

Point of contact
- Substitute $x = -2$ into $y = 2x + 7$ to find the y-coordinate of the point of contact.

HMRN: p. 40

Q6(*b*)

For circle C_1:

$x^2 + y^2 - 4x - 2y - 15 = 0$

Centre is: (2, 1) ✓

Radius $= \sqrt{2^2 + 1^2 - (-15)}$

$= \sqrt{4 + 1 + 15}$

$= \sqrt{20} = 2\sqrt{5}$ ✓

Now PQ is a diameter of C_2 ✓ with P(−2, 3) and Q(2, 1)

So $R\left(\frac{-2+2}{2}, \frac{3+1}{2}\right) = R(0, 2)$ ✓

The radius of C_2 is half the radius of C_1 i.e. $\frac{1}{2} \times 2\sqrt{5} = \sqrt{5}$ ✓

So the equation of C_2 is

$(x - 0)^2 + (y - 2)^2 = (\sqrt{5})^2$

$\Rightarrow x^2 + (y - 2)^2 = 5$ ✓

6 marks

Centre of C_1
- In the circle equation the coefficient of x is −4. Halve this and change the sign to get 2. This is the x-coordinate of the centre. Do a similar process to the y-coefficient −2.

Radius of C_1
- $\sqrt{20}$ gains this mark. $2\sqrt{5}$ is useful later.

Strategy
- The midpoint of a diameter is the centre.

Centre of C_2
- The midpoint of the line joining (x_1, y_1) and (x_2, y_2) is $\left(\frac{x_1 + x_2}{2}, \frac{y_1 + y_2}{2}\right)$.

Radius of C_2
- At this stage the form $2\sqrt{5}$ is easier to divide by 2 than $\sqrt{20}$.

Equation of C_2
- The equation of a circle with centre (a, b) and radius r is $(x - a)^2 + (y - b)^2 = r^2$. You are given this formula in the exam.

HMRN: p. 39

Q7

Shaded Area = Area under curve + Area of triangle ✓

Area under curve

$= \int_1^5 \left(1 - \frac{1}{\sqrt{2x-1}}\right) dx$ ✓

$= \int_1^5 \left(1 - (2x-1)^{-\frac{1}{2}}\right) dx$

$= \left[x - \frac{(2x-1)^{\frac{1}{2}}}{\frac{1}{2} \times 2}\right]_1^5 = \left[x - \sqrt{2x-1}\right]_1^5$ ✓ ✓ ✓

$= (5 - \sqrt{2 \times 5 - 1}) - (1 - \sqrt{2 \times 1 - 1})$

$= (5 - \sqrt{9}) - (1 - \sqrt{1})$ ✓

$= 5 - 3 - 1 + 1 = 2$ units^2

when $x = 5$

$y = -\frac{1}{15} \times 5 + 1 = -\frac{1}{3} + 1 = \frac{2}{3}$

Area of triangle

$= \frac{1}{2} \times$ base $\times$ height

$= \frac{1}{2} \times (15 - 5) \times \frac{2}{3}$

$= \frac{1}{2} \times 10 \times \frac{2}{3} = \frac{10}{3}$ units^2 ✓

Shaded area $= 2 + \frac{10}{3} = \frac{6}{3} + \frac{10}{3}$

$= \frac{16}{3}$ units^2 ✓

8 marks

Strategy

- Splitting the area into two pieces is essential: from $x = 1$ to $x = 5$ involves an integration but the area from $x = 5$ to $x = 15$ is easier since it is a triangle.

Integral

- This mark is gained from evidence that you knew to integrate.

Constant term

- Integrating the constant 1 gives x. In general the result is $\int a\, dx = ax + c$ where a is a constant.

Start integration

- The 2nd term needs preparation: $(2x-1)^{-\frac{1}{2}}$.

Complete integration

- The result used is $\int (ax+b)^n dx = \frac{(ax+b)^{n+1}}{a(n+1)} + C$ and is sometimes known as a 'special integral'. Notice the appearance of the factor a in the denominator. In this question this factor is 2.

Limits and substitution

- The result is $\int_a^b f(x)\, dx = F(b) - F(a)$ where $F(x)$ is the result of integrating $f(x)$.

Area of triangle

- For the height put $x = 5$ in $y = -\frac{1}{15}x + 1$.

Shaded area

- Add the two areas for this final mark.

HMRN: p. 32–33, p. 49

Q8(*a*)

$\log_{\sqrt{a}} b = 2c$

$\Rightarrow (\sqrt{a})^{2c} = b$ ✓

$\Rightarrow (a^{\frac{1}{2}})^{2c} = b \Rightarrow a^{\frac{1}{2}\times 2c} = b$ ✓

$\Rightarrow a^c = b \Rightarrow \log_a b = c$ ✓

3 marks

Convert to exponential form

- The result used is:

  $\log_p q = r \Leftrightarrow p^r = q$
- This result is not given to you in the exam and it is sometimes easier to remember it by using a numerical example:

  $\log_{10} 100 = 2 \Leftrightarrow 10^2 = 100$

Converting to log form

- Two results are used here:

  $\sqrt{a} = a^{\frac{1}{2}}$ and $(a^m)^n = a^{mn}$
- You should know that $a^c = b$ leads to $\log_a b = c$.

Q8(*b*)

By part (*a*) above, $\log_{\sqrt{a}} b$ has twice the value of $\log_a b$ ($2c$ is twice c). ✓

Since $\log_5 7$ is equal to $\log_{\sqrt{25}} 7$ ✓ it therefore has twice the value of $\log_{25} 7$ so:

$\log_5 7 - \log_{25} 7 = 2\log_{25} 7 - \log_{25} 7$

$= \log_{25} 7$ as required. ✓

3 marks

Strategy

- The crucial facts are the meaning of $2c$ and c for the relationship of the values of $\log_{\sqrt{a}} b$ and $\log_a b$ (twice the value), and also the fact that $5 = \sqrt{25}$ so that the result in part (*a*) can be used in this numerical case.

Start proof

- Stating $\log_5 7 = \log_{\sqrt{25}} 7$ should gain you this mark.

Complete proof

- The essential final step is stating:

  $\log_{\sqrt{25}} 7 = 2\log_{25} 7$

  and stating:

  $2\log_{25} 7 - \log_{25} 7 = \log_{25} 7$.

HMRN: p. 50–51

Q1

$x^2 + y^2 - 2x + 4y + 1 = 0$

Centre: $(1, -2)$

Radius

$= \sqrt{1^2 + (-2)^2 - 1} = \sqrt{1 + 4 - 1}$

$= \sqrt{4} = 2$

Choice B.

2 marks

- The process is:

$x^2 + y^2 + ax \quad + \quad by \quad + \quad c = 0$

halve and change sign

Centre: $\left(-\frac{a}{2}, \quad -\frac{b}{2}\right)$

square and add subtract

Radius $= \sqrt{\left(-\frac{a}{2}\right)^2 + \left(-\frac{b}{2}\right)^2 - c}$

So first halve the coefficients of x and y and change their sign to obtain the centre. Then square the coordinates of the centre, add the result then subtract the constant at the end of the circle equation. Take the square root of the result to get the radius.

HMRN: p. 39

Q2

$u_{n+1} = 5 - 2u_n$, $u_1 = 3$

So $u_2 = 5 - 2u_1 = 5 - 2 \times 3$

$= 5 - 6 = -1$

and $u_3 = 5 - 2u_2 = 5 - 2 \times (-1)$

$= 5 + 2 = 7$

Choice C.

2 marks

- A diagram may help:

u_1 → u_2 → u_3

Double then subtract from 5 $(5 - 2u_1)$; Double then subtract from 5 $(5 - 2u_2)$

3 → −1 → 7

$5 - 2 \times 3$; $5 - 2 \times (-1)$

HMRN: p. 23

Q3

P(−1, 3), Q(−2, 0)

$PQ = \sqrt{(-1-(-2))^2 + (3-0)^2}$

$= \sqrt{1^2 + 3^2} = \sqrt{1+9} = \sqrt{10}$

Choice B.

2 marks

- The distance formula is:

$AB = \sqrt{(x_1 - x_2)^2 + (y_1 - y_2)^2}$

where $A(x_1, y_1)$ and $B(x_2, y_2)$

- The pattern is:

Distance $= \sqrt{(x\text{– difference})^2 + (y\text{– difference})^2}$

HMRN: p. 7

Q4

A(−1, 0), B(1, 4)

$m_{AB} = \frac{4-0}{1-(-1)} = \frac{4}{2} = 2$

Choice D.

2 marks

- The gradient formula is:

$m_{AB} = \frac{y_2 - y_1}{x_2 - x_1}$ where $A(x_1, y_1)$ and $B(x_2, y_2)$

- The pattern is:

Gradient $= \frac{y \text{ difference}}{x \text{ difference}}$

- Note the order is important:

either $\frac{4-0}{1-(-1)}$ or $\frac{0-4}{-1-1}$

$\left(\frac{4}{2} = 2\right) \quad \left(\frac{-4}{-2} = 2\right)$

but *not* $\frac{4-0}{-1-1}$ or $\frac{0-4}{1-(-1)}$

$\left(\frac{4}{-2} = -2\right) \quad \left(\frac{-4}{2} = -2\right)$

HMRN: p. 3

Q5

$y = 3x - 2x^3$

$\Rightarrow \dfrac{dy}{dx} = 3 - 6x^2$

when $x = 2$, $\dfrac{dy}{dx} = 3 - 6 \times 2^2 = -21$

Choice A.

2 marks

- Results used are:

  $y = ax \Rightarrow \dfrac{dy}{dx} = a$

  $y = ax^n \Rightarrow \dfrac{dy}{dx} = anx^{n-1}$

- Remember to find the gradient of the tangent to a curve you need to differentiate.

HMRN: p. 20

Q6

$f(x) = \dfrac{2}{3x^2} = \dfrac{2x^{-2}}{3} = \dfrac{2}{3}x^{-2}$

$f'(x) = -2 \times \dfrac{2}{3}x^{-3} = -\dfrac{4}{3}x^{-3} = -\dfrac{4}{3x^3}$

Choice D.

2 marks

- $\dfrac{2}{3x^2}$ needs to be 'prepared' for differentiation.

  The x^2 has to be moved to the top of the fraction and changed to x^{-2}. The index law used is $x^{-n} = \dfrac{1}{x^n}$.

- Note that the coefficient 3 remains on the bottom of the fraction. Think of it like this:

  $\dfrac{2}{3x^2} = \dfrac{2}{3} \times \dfrac{1}{x^2} = \dfrac{2}{3} \times x^{-2} = \dfrac{2x^{-2}}{3}$

- To differentiate the result used is:

  $f(x) = ax^n \Rightarrow f'(x) = anx^{n-1}$

  You multiply by the index then subtract 1 from the index.

- $\dfrac{2x^{-2}}{3}$ and $\dfrac{2}{3}x^{-2}$ are the same as are, for example, $\dfrac{2}{3}a$ and $\dfrac{2a}{3}$ or $\dfrac{1}{2}x$ and $\dfrac{x}{2}$ etc.

- A common mistake is to think that subtracting 1 from −2 gives −1 and not −3. Think of the number line:

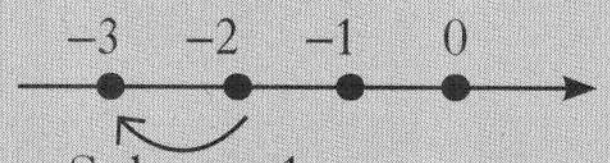

HMRN: p. 18

Q7

$u_{n+1} = 0{\cdot}85\, u_n + 1{\cdot}5$

Since the multiplier, 0·85, lies between 0 and 1 there is a limit, L say

$\Rightarrow L = 0{\cdot}85L + 1{\cdot}5$

$\Rightarrow L - 0{\cdot}85L = 1{\cdot}5$

$\Rightarrow 0{\cdot}15L = 1{\cdot}5$

$\Rightarrow L = \dfrac{1{\cdot}5}{0{\cdot}15} = \dfrac{150}{15} = 10$

Since $u_0 = 2{\cdot}5$ which is less than 10 and the limit is 10, no term of the sequence can be greater than 10 so statement (1) is not correct. Statement (2) is also not correct.

Choice A.

2 marks

- For a recurrence relation $u_{n+1} = au_n + b$ the condition for a limit to exist is $-1 < a < 1$, i.e. the multiplier a is some fractional value lying between −1 and 1.

- For $u_{n+1} = au_n + b$ the limit $L = \dfrac{b}{1-a}$ when $-1 < a < 1$. This formula is not given to you in the exam. You should know how to do the 'algebra' to find the limit as demonstrated in the working opposite.

HMRN: p. 24

Q8

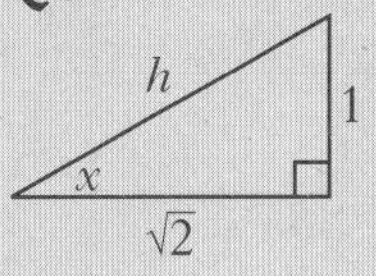

$h^2 = (\sqrt{2})^2 + 1^2$

$\Rightarrow h^2 = 2 + 1 = 3$

$\Rightarrow h = \sqrt{3}$

So $\sin x = \frac{1}{\sqrt{3}}$ and $\cos x = \frac{\sqrt{2}}{\sqrt{3}}$

$\sin 2x = 2 \sin x \cos x$

$= 2 \times \frac{1}{\sqrt{3}} \times \frac{\sqrt{2}}{\sqrt{3}} = \frac{2\sqrt{2}}{3}$

Choice C.

2 marks

- Given an exact value of $\sin x$, $\cos x$ or $\tan x$ you can always construct a right-angled triangle to fit the given value if $0 < x < \frac{\pi}{2}$. You then use Pythagoras' Theorem to determine the exact value of the third side. The two remaining exact values of $\sin x$, $\cos x$ or $\tan x$ can then be written down using SOHCAHTOA in the triangle.

HMRN: p. 35–36

Q9

$y = \log_3(x - 1)$.

The graph with this equation is obtained from the graph $y = \log_3 x$ by shifting it 1unit to the right (parallel to the x-axis).

Choice A.

2 marks

- You should know the following graph transformations for a positive constant k
  $y = f(x + k)$ moves $y = f(x)$ k units left
  $y = f(x - k)$ moves $y = f(x)$ k units right
  with these moves being parallel to the x-axis.
- You should double-check that the given points on the graph have x and y-coordinates that satisfy the equation of the graph. In this case:

(2, 0) $x = 2$, $y = 0$ gives $0 = \log_3(2 - 1)$

$\Rightarrow 0 = \log_3 1 \Rightarrow 3^0 = 1$ true ✓

(4, 1) $x = 4$, $y = 1$ gives $1 = \log_3(4 - 1)$

$\Rightarrow 1 = \log_3 3 \Rightarrow 3^1 = 3$ true ✓

HMRN: p. 13

Q10

$2\sin x\,(2\cos x - 3) = 0$

$\Rightarrow \sin x = 0$ or $2\cos x - 3 = 0$

$\Rightarrow \cos x = \frac{3}{2}$

For $\sin x = 0$ in the range $0 \le x < 2\pi$,

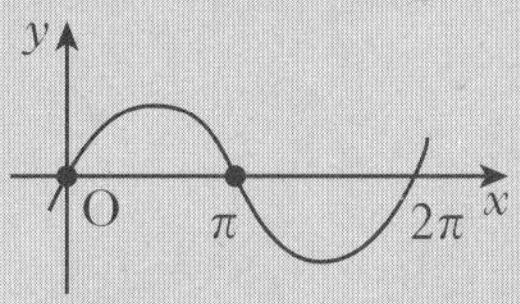

there are two solutions: $x = 0$ or $x = \pi$ as shown in the graph.

For $\cos x = \frac{3}{2}$ there are no solutions since the maximum value of $\cos x$ is 1.

Choice B.

2 marks

- You should be able to draw the sine, cosine and tangent graphs from memory as they are not given to you in the exam. In Paper 1 you cannot use a calculator.
- The range of values of x is crucial:

for $0 < x < 2\pi$ only $x = \pi$ is valid,
for $0 \le x \le 2\pi$ both $x = 0$ and $x = 2\pi$ are also valid in addition to $x = \pi$,

for $0 < x \le 2\pi$ $x = \pi$ and $x = 2\pi$ are valid but $x = 0$ is not.

- For $\cos x = \frac{3}{2}$.

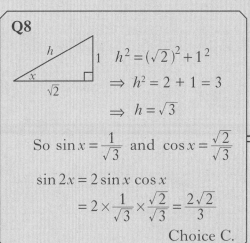

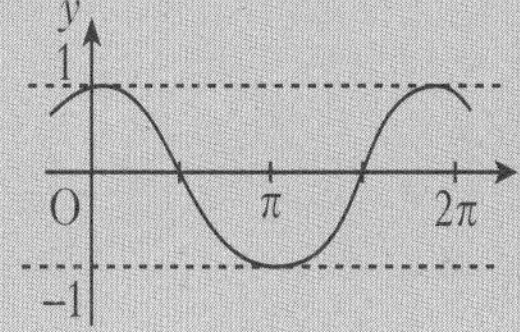

All points on the graph $y = \cos x$ lie between or on the two dotted lines in the graph diagram, so $-1 \le y \le 1$, i.e. $-1 \le \cos x \le 1$.

A y-coordinate value of $\frac{3}{2}$ for a point on the graph is not possible.

HMRN: p. 34, p. 37

Q11

For points of intersection

solve: $\left.\begin{array}{l} y=-x \\ x^2+y^2=4 \end{array}\right\} \Rightarrow x^2+(-x)^2=4$

$\Rightarrow 2x^2=4$

$\Rightarrow x^2=2$

$\Rightarrow x=\pm\sqrt{2}$

So $x_P=\sqrt{2}$ and $x_Q=-\sqrt{2}$

Choice D.

2 marks

- You can confirm that your selected values make sense by drawing a sketch:

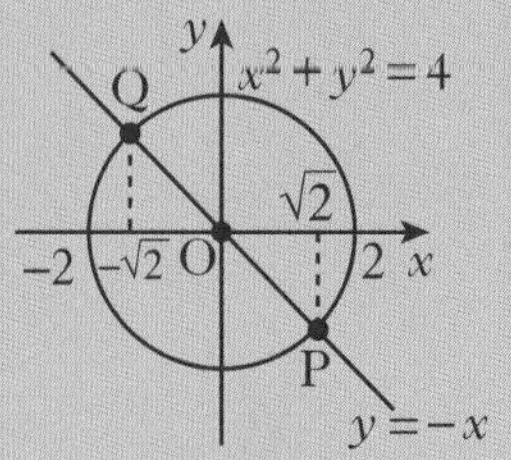

The two points of intersection support the values

$x_P=\sqrt{2}$ and $x_Q=-\sqrt{2}$

i.e. $x_P \doteqdot 1{\cdot}4 \quad x_Q \doteqdot -1{\cdot}4$

HMRN: p. 40

Q12

$f(x)=g(x)$

$\Rightarrow \sqrt{2}\sin\frac{1}{2}x+2=k$

$\Rightarrow \sqrt{2}\sin\frac{1}{2}x=k-2$

$\Rightarrow \sin\frac{1}{2}x=\frac{k-2}{\sqrt{2}}$

There is no solution if

$\frac{k-2}{\sqrt{2}}>1$ or if $\frac{k-2}{\sqrt{2}}<-1$

Now $\frac{k-2}{\sqrt{2}}>1 \Rightarrow k-2>\sqrt{2}$

$\Rightarrow k>\sqrt{2}+2 \Rightarrow k>2+\sqrt{2}$

Choice D.

2 marks

- Remember that the values of the sine of an angle take values from −1 to 1 including −1 and 1.

  The form of $\sin\frac{1}{2}x=\frac{k-2}{\sqrt{2}}$ is sin (angle) = constant so if this constant is greater than 1 or less than −1 there will be no angle whose sine will give this value, i.e. there will be no solution to the equation.

- It is possible to solve this question by sketching the graph $y=\sqrt{2}\sin\frac{1}{2}x+2$.

  This is a single graph with amplitude $\sqrt{2}$ and period 4π shifted up parallel to the y-axis by 2 units:

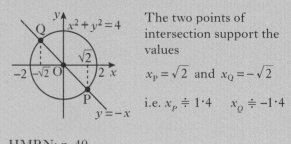

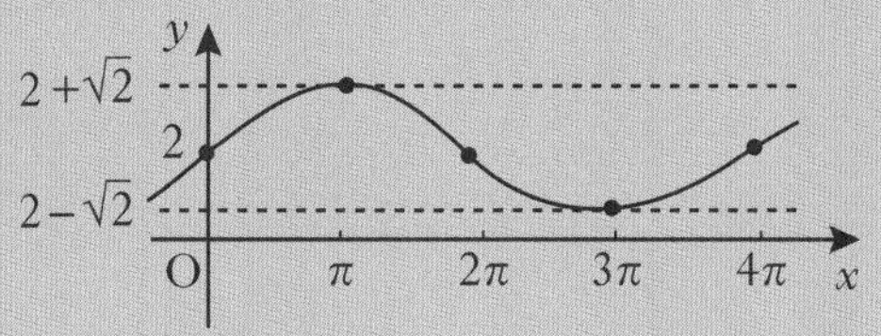

As can be seen, the values of $\sqrt{2}\sin\frac{1}{2}x+2$ lie between or are equal to $2-\sqrt{2}$ and $2+\sqrt{2}$.

So if $k>2+\sqrt{2}$ there are no solutions.

HMRN: p. 15–17

Q13

for $9m^2-3m-2=0$

The discriminant

$=(-3)^2-4\times9\times(-2)$

$=9+72=81$

Since discriminant > 0 there are two distinct real roots.

Also 81 is a perfect square since $81=9^2$ so the two roots will be rational.

Choice D.

2 marks

- Compare $9m^2-3m-2=0$

  with $am^2+bm+c=0$

  The discriminant b^2-4ac is calculated using the values $a=9$, $b=-3$ and $c=-2$

- Be very careful with negative signs. Both b and c have negative values.

  Squaring negative values always gives a positive value. Also the term $-4\times9\times(-2)$ gives + 72.

- The quadratic formula for $am^2+bm+c=0$ gives $m=\frac{-b\pm\sqrt{b^2-4ac}}{2a}$. When b^2-4ac is a perfect square there is no need for a square root sign: in this case $\sqrt{81}=9$ and the values of m are $\frac{3\pm9}{18}$ i.e. $\frac{12}{18}$ and $-\frac{6}{18}$ i.e. $\frac{2}{3}$ and $-\frac{1}{3}$, both rational values (no surds!)

HMRN: p. 27

Q14

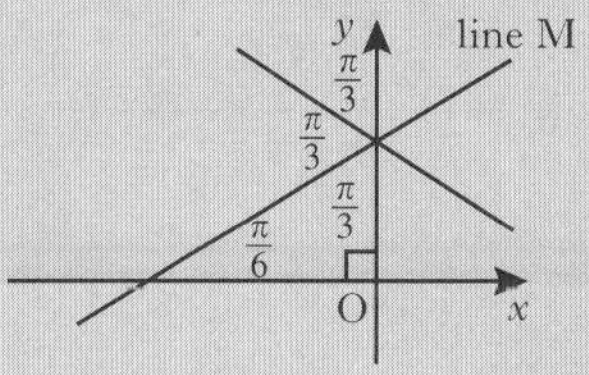

gradient of line M $= \tan\frac{\pi}{6}$

$= \frac{1}{\sqrt{3}}$

Choice B.

2 marks

- The result used is: gradient of line $= \tan\theta$

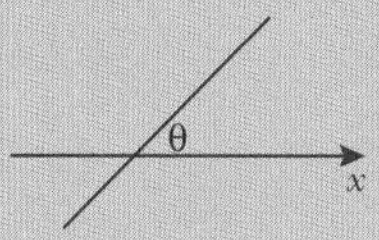

- Exact value of $\tan\frac{\pi}{6}$ can be calculated from the 'half an equilateral triangle' diagram.

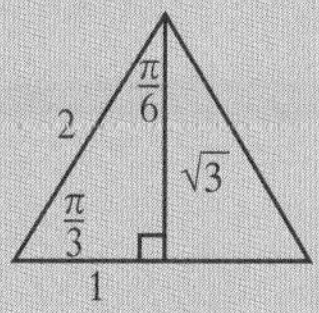

HMRN: p. 4

Q15

$\frac{R\sin\theta}{R\cos\theta} = \frac{\sqrt{3}}{\sqrt{3}} \Rightarrow \tan\theta = 1 \Rightarrow \theta = \frac{\pi}{4}$

also $(R\sin\theta)^2 + (R\cos\theta)^2$

$= (\sqrt{3})^2 + (\sqrt{3})^2$

$\Rightarrow R^2\sin^2\theta + R^2\cos^2\theta = 3 + 3$

$\Rightarrow R^2(\sin^2\theta + \cos^2\theta) = 6$

$\Rightarrow R^2 \times 1 = 6 \Rightarrow R^2 = 6$

$\Rightarrow R = \sqrt{6} \quad (R > 0)$

Choice A.

2 marks

- Two trigonometrical identities that you learnt in your previous course are used here:

  $\frac{\sin\theta}{\cos\theta} = \tan\theta$ and $\sin^2\theta + \cos^2\theta = 1$

  These identities are not on your formulae sheet for the exam and you need to learn them.
- The exact value $\tan\frac{\pi}{4} = 1$ can be calculated from the 'half a square' diagram.

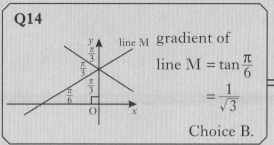

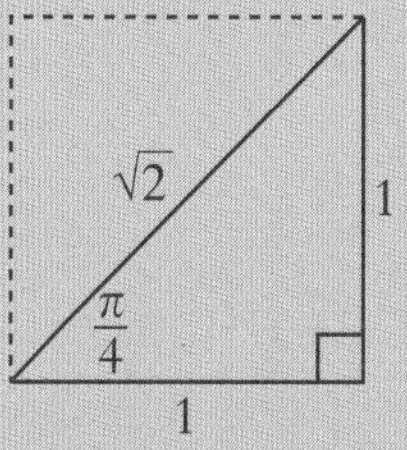

- You will recognise this question as a calculation that you need to do when you are, for example, writing $2\sin x - 3\cos x$ as $R\sin(x - \theta)$. This is an area of the course referred to as 'the wave function'.

HMRN: p. 53–54

Q16

$f(x) = \frac{2}{\sqrt{1-3x}} = \frac{2}{(1-3x)^{\frac{1}{2}}}$

$= 2(1-3x)^{-\frac{1}{2}}$

$\Rightarrow f'(x) = -\frac{1}{2} \times 2(1-3x)^{-\frac{3}{2}} \times (-3)$

$= 3(1-3x)^{-\frac{3}{2}}$

Choice A.

2 marks

- You first have to prepare $\frac{2}{\sqrt{1-3x}}$ for differentiation. The results you are using are:

  $\sqrt{a} = a^{\frac{1}{2}}$ and $a^{-n} = \frac{1}{a^n}$.

  The expression is 'ready' when it is in the form $a(f(x))^n$.
- The chain rule is used. In this form it is:

  $y = a(f(x))^n \Rightarrow \frac{dy}{dx} = an(f(x))^{n-1} \times f'(x)$

  with $f(x) = 1 - 3x$ giving $f'(x) = -3$ as the 'chain rule' factor.
- For the index:

  $-\frac{1}{2} - 1 = -\frac{1}{2} - \frac{2}{2} = \frac{-1-2}{2} = \frac{-3}{2} = -\frac{3}{2}$.

HMRN: p. 48–49

Q17

$\int -x^2\,dx = -\frac{x^3}{3} + C$

This eliminates Choices C and D. Since the shaded area is below the x-axis $\left[-\frac{x^3}{3}\right]_{-1}^{1}$ will give the negative of the required area. So not Choice B.

This leaves Choice A.

2 marks

- The basic result is: Shaded area
  $= \int_a^b f(x)\,dx$
  $= [F(x)]_a^b$
  $= F(b) - F(a)$

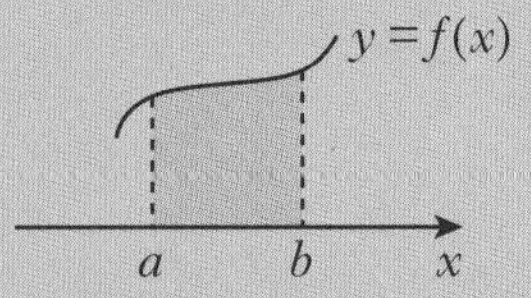

  where F(x) is the result of integrating $f(x)$.
- There is symmetry about the y-axis so $-\left[-\frac{x^3}{3}\right]_{-1}^{0}$ and $-\left[-\frac{x^3}{3}\right]_{0}^{1}$ are equal and give the shaded areas to the left and right of the y-axis respectively.

  So $2\times\left(-\left[-\frac{x^3}{3}\right]_0^1\right)$ is the required area, i.e. $-2\left[-\frac{x^3}{3}\right]_0^1$.

  HMRN: p. 32

Q18

$\boldsymbol{v}$ and $\boldsymbol{u}$ are unit vectors

So $|\boldsymbol{v}| = 1$ and $|\boldsymbol{u}| = 1$

Now the result $\boldsymbol{u}.\boldsymbol{v} = |\boldsymbol{u}||\boldsymbol{v}|\cos\theta$ where θ is the angle between $\boldsymbol{u}$ and $\boldsymbol{v}$ can be rearranged to:

$\cos\theta = \frac{\boldsymbol{u}.\boldsymbol{v}}{|\boldsymbol{u}||\boldsymbol{v}|}$ and since they are perpendicular vectors.

$\cos\theta = \cos\frac{\pi}{2} = 0$ so $\frac{\boldsymbol{u}.\boldsymbol{v}}{|\boldsymbol{u}||\boldsymbol{v}|} = 0$

Choice B.

2 marks

- A fact you should know is that if $\boldsymbol{a}$ and $\boldsymbol{b}$ are perpendicular then $\boldsymbol{a}.\boldsymbol{b} = 0$. In this case $\boldsymbol{u}.\boldsymbol{v} = 0$ and so choice A is not correct.
- For choice C: this tells you the magnitude of the difference of $\boldsymbol{u}$ and $\boldsymbol{v}$ is zero. If the magnitude of a vector is zero then it is the zero vector so this means $\boldsymbol{u} - \boldsymbol{v} = \boldsymbol{0} \Rightarrow \boldsymbol{u} = \boldsymbol{v}$ but two perpendicular vectors cannot be equal. Choice C is not correct.
- Since $|\boldsymbol{u}| = 1$ and $|\boldsymbol{v}| = 1$, Choice D gives $\frac{\boldsymbol{v}.\boldsymbol{u}}{|\boldsymbol{v}||\boldsymbol{u}|} = 1 \Rightarrow \frac{\boldsymbol{v}.\boldsymbol{u}}{1\times 1} = 1 \Rightarrow \boldsymbol{v}.\boldsymbol{u} = 1$ and this is ruled out for the reasons given above for ruling out Choice A.

  HMRN: p. 46–47

Q19

$$V(r) = \frac{2}{3}\pi r^3 + \pi r^2$$
$$\Rightarrow V'(r) = 3\times\frac{2}{3}\pi r^2 + 2\pi r^1$$
$$= 2\pi r^2 + 2\pi r$$
$$= 2\pi r\,(r+1)$$
$$\text{So } V'\left(\frac{1}{2}\right) = 2\pi\times\frac{1}{2}\times\left(\frac{1}{2}+1\right)$$
$$= \pi\left(\frac{3}{2}\right) = \frac{3\pi}{2}$$

Choice C.

2 marks

- The complications in this question are:
  The variable used is r not x.
  π appears in the expression.
  The function is called V not f.
  Let's change the variable to x and the function name to f:
  $$f(x) = \frac{2}{3}\pi x^3 + \pi x^2$$
  Now π is approximately 3 so $\frac{2}{3}\pi$ is approximately 2, so using these rough values you get: $f(x) = 2x^3 + 3x^2$ giving $f'(x) = 3\times 2x^2 + 2\times 3x$.

  Compare $V'(r) = 3\times\frac{2}{3}\pi\times r^2 + 2\times\pi r$ as in line two of the working.

  HMRN: p. 22

Q20

$1 < 4t^2$

$\Rightarrow 4t^2 > 1$

$\Rightarrow 4t^2 - 1 > 0$

Now consider the graph

$y = 4t^2 - 1 = (2t - 1)(2t + 1)$

t-axis intercepts are given by setting $y = 0$ so $(2t - 1)(2t + 1) = 0$

$\Rightarrow 2t - 1 = 0$ or $2t + 1 = 0$

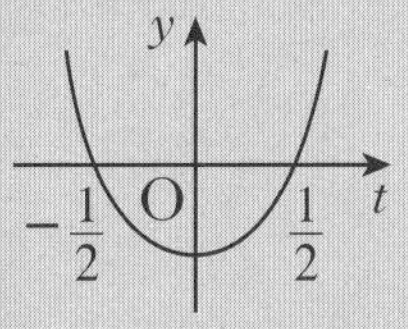

$\Rightarrow t = \frac{1}{2}$ or $t = -\frac{1}{2}$

So $4t^2 - 1 > 0$

when $t < -\frac{1}{2}$ or $t > \frac{1}{2}$

Choice C.

2 marks

- Remember that when you are looking at a graph like $y = 4t^2 - 1$, then it is the heights of points on the graph that tell you whether $4t^2 - 1$ is positive, zero or negative. Solving $4t^2 - 1 > 0$ requires you to find values for t that give corresponding points on the graph that are above the t-axis. This gives the branch of the curve to the right of $t = \frac{1}{2}$ and the branch to the left of $t = -\frac{1}{2}$. This leads to $t > \frac{1}{2}$ and $t < -\frac{1}{2}$. Note you cannot include $t = \frac{1}{2}$ or $t = -\frac{1}{2}$.

HMRN: p. 29

Q21(*a*)

$\overrightarrow{AB} = \boldsymbol{b} - \boldsymbol{a} = \begin{pmatrix} k \\ k \\ 0 \end{pmatrix} - \begin{pmatrix} 1 \\ -2 \\ -k \end{pmatrix} = \begin{pmatrix} k-1 \\ k+2 \\ k \end{pmatrix}$

$\overrightarrow{AC} = \boldsymbol{c} - \boldsymbol{a} = \begin{pmatrix} 4 \\ -3 \\ 3-k \end{pmatrix} - \begin{pmatrix} 1 \\ -2 \\ -k \end{pmatrix} = \begin{pmatrix} 3 \\ -1 \\ 3 \end{pmatrix}$ ✓

since $\overrightarrow{AB}$ and $\overrightarrow{AC}$ are perpendicular

then $\overrightarrow{AB} \cdot \overrightarrow{AC} = 0 \Rightarrow \begin{pmatrix} k-1 \\ k+2 \\ k \end{pmatrix} \cdot \begin{pmatrix} 3 \\ -1 \\ 3 \end{pmatrix} = 0$ ✓

$\Rightarrow 3(k - 1) - 1(k + 2) + 3k = 0$ ✓

$\Rightarrow 3k - 3 - k - 2 + 3k = 0$

$\Rightarrow 5k - 5 = 0$

$\Rightarrow 5k = 5 \Rightarrow k = 1$ ✓

4 marks

Strategy

- The scalar product and the components of $\overrightarrow{AB}$ and $\overrightarrow{AC}$ are the ingredients of this vector approach.
- It is possible to use the distance formula and the fact that $AB^2 + AC^2 = BC^2$ to find k.

Scalar product = 0

- If $\boldsymbol{v}$ and $\boldsymbol{u}$ are perpendicular then $\boldsymbol{u}.\boldsymbol{v} = 0$.

Calculation

- $\begin{pmatrix} x_1 \\ y_1 \\ z_1 \end{pmatrix} \cdot \begin{pmatrix} x_2 \\ y_2 \\ z_2 \end{pmatrix} = x_1x_2 + y_1y_2 + z_1z_2$
- The appearance of $3(k - 1) - 1(k + 2) + 3k$ gains this mark.

Value

- Correctly solve the resulting equation to gain this final mark.
- Be careful with the term $(k + 2) \times (-1)$. Both parts of this term are multiplied by -1:

$k \times (-1)$ and $2 \times (-1)$ resulting in $-k - 2$.

HMRN: p. 46

Q21(*b*)

A(1, −2, −1), C(4, −3, 2) and D(13, −6, 11)

$\overrightarrow{AC} = \begin{pmatrix} 3 \\ -1 \\ 3 \end{pmatrix}$ from part (*a*) above

$\overrightarrow{CD} = \boldsymbol{d} - \boldsymbol{c} = \begin{pmatrix} 13 \\ -6 \\ 11 \end{pmatrix} - \begin{pmatrix} 4 \\ -3 \\ 2 \end{pmatrix} = \begin{pmatrix} 9 \\ -3 \\ 9 \end{pmatrix}$ ✓

So $\overrightarrow{CD} = 3\overrightarrow{AC}$ so $\overrightarrow{CD}$ and $\overrightarrow{AC}$ are parallel ✓ and since C is a shared point then A, C and D are collinear ✓

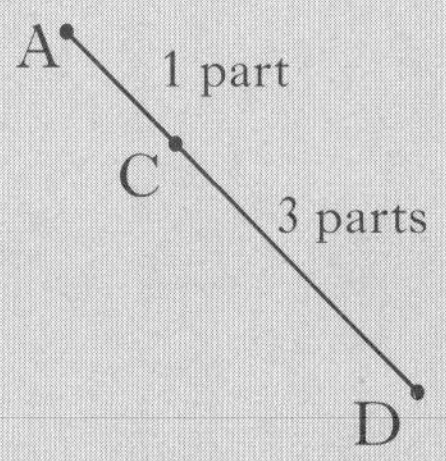

C divides AD in the ratio 1:3 ✓

4 marks

Strategy
- Determining the components of two directed line segments is required, e.g. $\overrightarrow{AC}$ and $\overrightarrow{CD}$ or $\overrightarrow{AD}$ and $\overrightarrow{CD}$ or $\overrightarrow{AC}$ and $\overrightarrow{AD}$ etc., providing the pair involves A, C and D.

Comparision
- Be careful when writing down the relationship since $\overrightarrow{CD} = 3\overrightarrow{AC}$ is different from $3\overrightarrow{CD} = \overrightarrow{AC}$.

Statement
- It is essential to state:

(1) The line segments are parallel.

(2) The line segments share a common point.

(3) The points are therefore collinear.

You will not gain this mark if you leave one of these three statements out of your solution.

Ratio
- A sketch showing the relationship $\overrightarrow{CD} = 3\overrightarrow{AC}$ helps to determine the correct ratio.
- 3:1 is not correct. This is the ratio in which C divides DA. In this context AD is different from DA and indicates the order for the ratio.

HMRN: p. 45

Q22(*a*)

R(1, −3) and Q(3, 5)

$$M\left(\frac{1+3}{2}, \frac{-3+5}{2}\right) = M(2,1) \checkmark$$

1 mark

Coordinates
- The midpoint of the line joining (x_1, y_1) and (x_2, y_2) is $\left(\frac{x_1+x_2}{2}, \frac{y_1+y_2}{2}\right)$

HMRN: p. 7

Q22(*b*)

P(−3, 1) and R(1, −3)

$\Rightarrow m_{PR} = \frac{1-(-3)}{-3-1} = \frac{4}{-4} = -1$ ✓

$\Rightarrow m_{\perp} = 1 \Rightarrow m_{MN} = 1$ ✓

A point on MN is M(2, 1) and the gradient = 1 so equation of MN is

$y - 1 = 1(x - 2) \Rightarrow y - 1 = x - 2$

$\Rightarrow y = x - 1$ ✓

3 marks

Gradient
- The gradient formula is used:

$$\text{gradient} = \frac{y - \text{difference}}{x - \text{difference}}$$

Strategy
- Altitude QT is perpendicular to side PR and so therefore is line MN since it is parallel to the altitude.
- The product of two perpendicular gradients is −1 (in this case 1 × (−1)).
- $m_{\perp}$ means "the gradient of a perpendicular line".

Equation
- You are using $y - b = m(x - a)$ where (a, b) is (2, 1) and $m = 1$.

HMRN: p. 4–6

Q22(c)

For the equation of PR:
A point on PR is P(−3, 1)
and the gradient = −1
so the equation is

$$y - 1 = -1(x - (-3))$$

$$\Rightarrow y - 1 = -x - 3 \Rightarrow y = -x - 2 \quad ✓$$

To find N solve:

$$\left.\begin{aligned} y &= x - 1 \\ y &= -x - 2 \end{aligned}\right\} \begin{aligned} &\Rightarrow x - 1 = -x - 2 \quad ✓ \\ &\Rightarrow x + x = 1 - 2 \\ &\Rightarrow 2x = -1 \\ &\Rightarrow x = -\frac{1}{2} \quad ✓ \end{aligned}$$

when $x = -\frac{1}{2}$, $y = -\frac{1}{2} - 1 = -\frac{3}{2}$ ✓

So $N\left(-\frac{1}{2}, -\frac{3}{2}\right)$

4 marks

Equation
- To find the intersection of MN and PR, the equation of PR needs to be found.

Strategy
- You are solving simultaneous equations to find N, the intersection of MN and PR.
- The nature of the equations, both of the form y = (an expression in x) allows you to set the two expressions in x equal to each other.
- Alternatively $y = x - 1 \Rightarrow y - x = -1$ and $y = -x - 2 \Rightarrow y + x = -2$ to get:

$$\left.\begin{aligned} y - x &= -1 \\ y + x &= -2 \end{aligned}\right\} \text{Now add these equations to get } 2y = -3$$

$$\Rightarrow y = -\frac{3}{2}$$

Now substitute $y = -\frac{3}{2}$ into $y + x = -2$ giving $-\frac{3}{2} + x = -2 \Rightarrow x = -2 + \frac{3}{2} = -\frac{1}{2}$.

The method given opposite is easier and less prone to errors.

***x*-coordinate**
1 mark for one of the coordinates.

***y*-coordinate**
1 mark for the other coordinate.

HMRN: p. 6

Q23(a)(i)

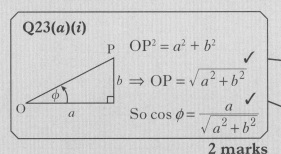

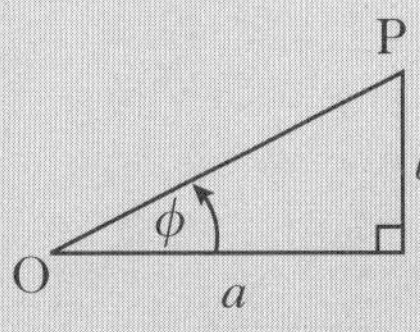

$OP^2 = a^2 + b^2$ ✓

$\Rightarrow OP = \sqrt{a^2 + b^2}$ ✓

So $\cos\phi = \frac{a}{\sqrt{a^2 + b^2}}$

2 marks

Strategy
- Use SOHCAHTOA in the right-angled triangle after finding the hypotenuse.

Result
- Cosine is Adjacent over Hypotenuse.

Q23(a)(ii)

$\sin\phi = \frac{b}{\sqrt{a^2 + b^2}}$ ✓

1 mark

Result
- Sine is Opposite over Hypotenuse.

Q23(b)(i)

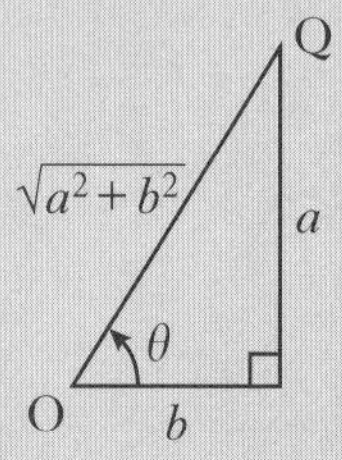

$\cos\theta = \dfrac{b}{\sqrt{a^2+b^2}}$ and $\sin\theta = \dfrac{a}{\sqrt{a^2+b^2}}$ ✓

$$\cos(\theta - \phi) = \cos\theta\cos\phi + \sin\theta\sin\phi \quad ✓$$
$$= \frac{b}{\sqrt{a^2+b^2}} \times \frac{a}{\sqrt{a^2+b^2}} + \frac{a}{\sqrt{a^2+b^2}} \times \frac{b}{\sqrt{a^2+b^2}} \quad ✓$$
$$= \frac{ab}{a^2+b^2} + \frac{ab}{a^2+b^2}$$
$$= \frac{2ab}{a^2+b^2} \quad ✓$$

4 marks

Sinθ, Cosθ expressions
- When dealing with Q(b, a) notice that the lengths of the shorter sides are swapped round compared to the triangle using P(a, b).

Expansion
- The following addition formula is given to you during your exam:

cos(A ± B) = cosA cosB ∓ sinA sinB

Substitution
- Be very careful – there are four different substitutions on the go: sinθ, cosθ, sinϕ and cosϕ. It is very easy to make errors!

Simplification
- Remember $\sqrt{x} \times \sqrt{x} = x$ so in this case $\sqrt{a^2+b^2} \times \sqrt{a^2+b^2} = a^2+b^2$. A mistake commonly made is to say $\sqrt{a^2+b^2} = a+b$. A numerical example shows this to be wrong: $\sqrt{3^2+4^2} = \sqrt{9+16} = \sqrt{25} = 5 \neq 3+4$.

Q23(b)(ii)

$$\sin(\theta - \phi) = \sin\theta\cos\phi - \cos\theta\sin\phi$$
$$= \frac{a}{\sqrt{a^2+b^2}} \times \frac{a}{\sqrt{a^2+b^2}} - \frac{b}{\sqrt{a^2+b^2}} \times \frac{b}{\sqrt{a^2+b^2}} \quad ✓$$
$$= \frac{a^2}{a^2+b^2} - \frac{b^2}{a^2+b^2}$$
$$= \frac{a^2-b^2}{a^2+b^2} \quad ✓$$

2 marks

Expansion & substitution
- Both the expansion and the substitution need to be correct to gain this mark.

Simplification
- One single fraction is required. There is no cancelling possible. $a^2 - b^2$ factorises into $(a - b)(a + b)$ but $a^2 + b^2$ does not factorise.

HMRN: p. 35

Q24(a)

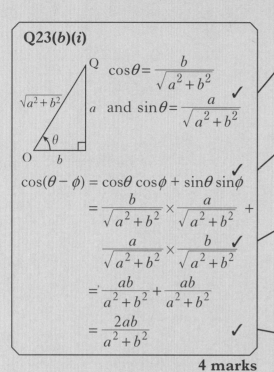

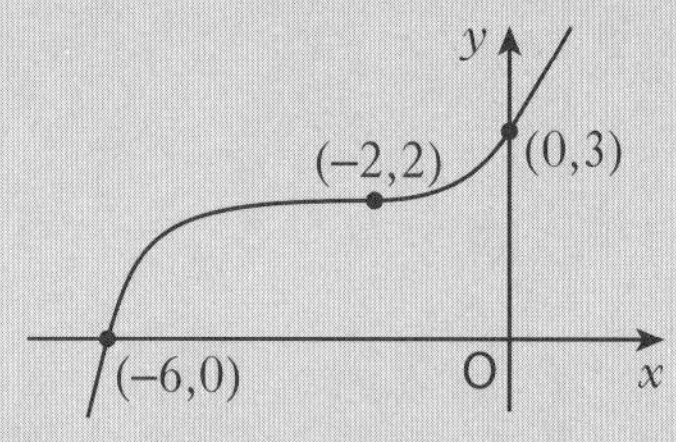

✓ ✓

2 marks

Scaling parallel to x-axis
- A more familiar example is to use $f(x) = \sin x$ and compare $y = f\left(\frac{1}{2}x\right) = \sin\frac{1}{2}x$. The graph is subjected to a 'horizontal stretching' so in this case $(-1, 2) \to (-2, 2)$ and $(-3, 0) \to (-6, 0)$.

Annotation
- One point correct for the 1st mark, the remaining two points correct for this 2nd mark.

Q24(*b*)

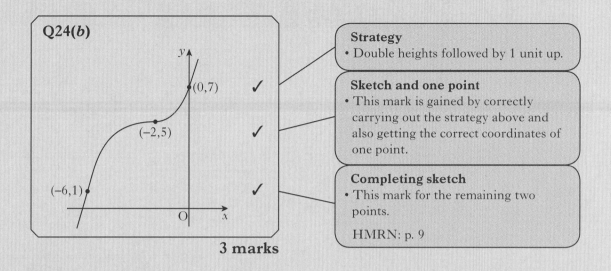

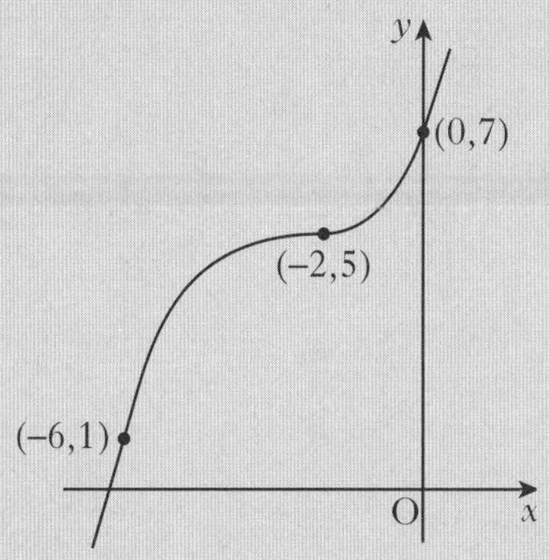

✓ ✓ ✓

3 marks

Strategy
- Double heights followed by 1 unit up.

Sketch and one point
- This mark is gained by correctly carrying out the strategy above and also getting the correct coordinates of one point.

Completing sketch
- This mark for the remaining two points.

HMRN: p. 9

Q1(*a*)

-3	6	13	-14	3
		-18	15	-3
	6	-5	1	0 ✓

Since $f(-3) = 0$ $x + 3$ is a factor. ✓

2 marks

Calculation
- The 'synthetic division' scheme uses the coefficients in the polynomial. You should watch for negatives (-14 in this case) or for missing terms (all terms are present in this case) in which case a zero is used.

Statement
- Mention must be made of this calculation producing a zero and hence $x + 3$ is a factor. The result is:

$f(a) = 0 \Leftrightarrow a$ is a root $\Leftrightarrow x - a$ is a factor.

Q1(*b*)

$f(x) = (x + 3)(6x^2 - 5x + 1)$ ✓ ✓

$= (x + 3)(2x - 1)(3x - 1)$ ✓

3 marks

Start factorisation
- Appearance of: $(x + 3)(6x^2 - ....)$

Quadratic factor
- This mark is for $6x^2 - 5x + 1$.

Factorise fully
- The three factors must appear multiplied together, i.e. $(x + 3)(2x - 1)(3x - 1)$ to gain this final mark.

HMRN: p. 26

Q2

$y = 2x^3 - x^2 + 1$ ✓

$\Rightarrow \dfrac{dy}{dx} = 6x^2 - 2x$ ✓

For stationary points set $\dfrac{dy}{dx} = 0$ ✓

$\Rightarrow 6x^2 - 2x = 0$

$\Rightarrow 2x(3x - 1) = 0$ ✓

$\Rightarrow x = 0$ or $3x - 1 = 0$

$\Rightarrow x = \dfrac{1}{3}$ ✓

x:		0		$\frac{1}{3}$	
$\dfrac{dy}{dx} = 2x(3x-1)$:	+		−		+ ✓
Shape of graph:	/	max	\	min	/ ✓

When $x = 0$ $y = 2 \times 0^3 - 0^2 + 1 = 1$

So (0, 1) is a maximum stationary point.

When $x = \dfrac{1}{3}$ $y = 2 \times \left(\dfrac{1}{3}\right)^3 - \left(\dfrac{1}{3}\right)^2 + 1$

$= \dfrac{2}{27} - \dfrac{1}{9} + 1$

$= \dfrac{2}{27} - \dfrac{3}{27} + \dfrac{27}{27}$

$= \dfrac{2 - 3 + 27}{27} = \dfrac{26}{27}$ ✓

So $\left(\dfrac{1}{3}, \dfrac{26}{27}\right)$ is a minimum stationary point.

8 marks

Strategy
- Stationary points occur where the gradient is zero so the strategy is to differentiate.

Differentiate
- This mark is for $6x^2 - 2x$.
- Note: differentiating a constant, in this case 1, gives zero. This is why 1 vanishes!

Derivative is zero
- It is important that "= 0" occurs to gain this mark.

Factorisation
- Recognise that you have a quadratic equation to solve and so this leads to you factorising the expression $6x^2 - 2x$.

Solutions
- There are two solutions, $x = 0$ and $x = \frac{1}{3}$, each giving a stationary point on the curve.

Justify nature
- For this mark your 'nature table' should clearly show the labels "x:" and "$\frac{dy}{dx}$".

Interpretation
- You must clearly link "min" and "max" with the appropriate points.

***y*-coordinates**
- Take care over this calculation. You do have use of your calculator for this. Sometimes these are fairly complicated calculations.

HMRN: p. 20–21

Q3(*a*)

$f(g(x)) = f(2x+1)$ ✓

$= \dfrac{2}{(2x+1)+1} = \dfrac{2}{2x+2}$ ✓

$= \dfrac{2}{2(x+1)} = \dfrac{1}{x+1}$

Also $\dfrac{1}{2}f(x) = \dfrac{1}{2} \times \dfrac{2}{x+1}$

$= \dfrac{2}{2(x+1)} = \dfrac{1}{x+1}$ ✓

So $f(2x+1) = \dfrac{1}{2}f(x)$ ✓

4 marks

Strategy

- The essence of the method is to simplify $f(g(x))$ and $\frac{1}{2}f(x)$ separately and so reduce them to the same expression $\left(\text{i.e. } \frac{1}{x+1}\right)$.

***f*(*g*(*x*))**

- The expression $\frac{2}{x+1}$ requires x to be replaced by the expression for $g(x)$, i.e. $2x + 1$ as a first stage.
- $(2x + 1) + 1$ needs to be simplified.
- This mark would be gained for $\frac{2}{2x+2}$

$\frac{1}{2}f(x)$

- Either $\frac{2}{2(x+1)}$ or $\frac{1}{x+1}$ or $\frac{2}{2x+2}$.

Proof

- Reduction to the same expression is required. You will not gain this mark if you have $\frac{2}{2x+2}$ for $f(g(x))$ and $\frac{2}{2(x+1)}$ for $\frac{1}{2}f(x)$.

  They are both equal either to $\frac{2}{2x+2}$ or to $\frac{2}{2(x+1)}$ or to $\frac{1}{x+1}$ but not to two different forms.

HMRN: p. 10

Q3(*b*)

$g(x) = 2x + 1$

$\Rightarrow g'(x) = 2$ ✓

So $\dfrac{g'(x)}{f(x)} = \dfrac{2}{\frac{2}{x+1}}$

$= \dfrac{2 \times (x+1)}{\frac{2}{x+1} \times (x+1)}$

$= \dfrac{2(x+1)}{2} = x+1$ ✓

2 marks

Differentiate

- If, for example, $p(x) = ax + b$ where a and b are constants, then $p'(x) = a$. In this case $a = 2$ and $b = 1$.

Simplification

- The alternative 'invert and multiply' can be used for $2 \div \frac{2}{x+1}$ to give $2 \times \frac{x+1}{2}$ with the factor 2 then being cancelled.
- Leaving this as a 'double decker' fraction, i.e. a fraction with another fraction on the top or bottom, is not considered simplified.

HMRN: p. 18

Q4(*a*)

$f(x) = \sin 2x + 1$

and $g(x) = \sin x + 1$

So $a = 2$, $b = 1$, $c = 1$ and $d = 1$ ✓

1 mark

Interpretation

- You are using the following general result:

$k\sin ax + b$

amplitude → k; number of cycles from 0 to 2π → a; 'vertical' shift → b

- You are not concerned here with any amplitude changes, only the number of cycles (or period) and a y-axis (or vertical) shift.

HMRN: p. 16

Q4(*b*)

To find the points of intersection

Solve: $\sin 2x + 1 = \sin x + 1$ ✓

$\Rightarrow \sin 2x - \sin x = 0$

$\Rightarrow 2\sin x \cos x - \sin x = 0$

$\Rightarrow \sin x\,(2\cos x - 1) = 0$

$\Rightarrow \sin x = 0$ or $\cos x = \frac{1}{2}$

For $\sin x = 0$, $x = 0, \pi, 2\pi, \ldots$
In the range $0 < x \leq \pi$ this gives B. ✓

For $\cos x = \frac{1}{2}$, x is in the 1st or 4th quadrant, however only the 1st quadrant angle is in the range $0 < x \leq \pi$ ✓

so $x = \frac{\pi}{3}$ is the required exact value. ✓

4 marks

Strategy
- To find the x-coordinate values of the points of intersection you set the two curve equations equal to each other and then solve.

Solve equation
- The double angle formula is used to change the form of the equation so that factorisation can be done.
- On your formula sheet is: $\sin 2A = 2\sin A \cos A$.
- The common factor is $\sin x$.

Identification of point
- It should be clear from the graph that the required x-value gives a 1st quadrant angle.

Exact value
- $\cos x = \frac{1}{2}$ leads to consideration of the following triangle:

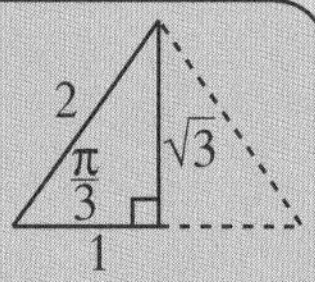

This triangle is half of an equilateral triangle with side length 2 units. SOHCAHTOA identifies the required angle as $\frac{\pi}{3}$.

HMRN: p. 37

Q4(*c*) ✓

Shaded area

$= \int_{\frac{\pi}{3}}^{\pi} (\sin x + 1) - (\sin 2x + 1)\,dx$ ✓

$= \int_{\frac{\pi}{3}}^{\pi} \sin x - \sin 2x\,dx$ ✓

$= \left[-\cos x + \frac{\cos 2x}{2}\right]_{\frac{\pi}{3}}^{\pi}$ ✓

$= \left(-\cos \pi + \frac{\cos 2\pi}{2}\right) - \left(-\cos\frac{\pi}{3} + \frac{\cos\frac{2\pi}{3}}{2}\right)$ ✓

$= \left(-(-1) + \frac{1}{2}\right) - \left(-\frac{1}{2} + \frac{\left(-\frac{1}{2}\right)}{2}\right)$

$= 1 + \frac{1}{2} + \frac{1}{2} + \frac{1}{4}$

$= 2\frac{1}{4}$ units^2 ✓

6 marks

Strategy
- The result used is:

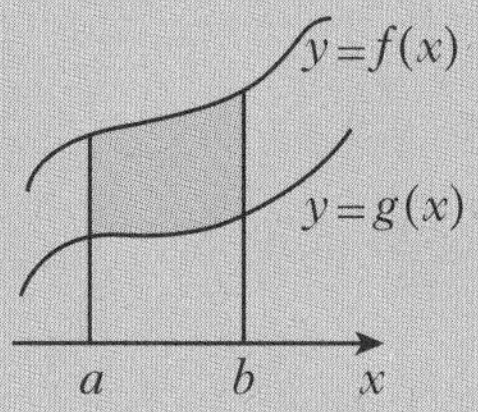

shaded area
$= \int_a^b f(x) - g(x)\,dx$

top curve ↗ bottom curve ↖

- Remember to put brackets round the expression $\sin 2x + 1$. $-(\sin 2x + 1)$ is correct, $-\sin 2x + 1$ is wrong.

Limits
- From part (*b*) you have determined $\frac{\pi}{3}$ as the lower limit (left). π is the upper limit (right).

Integration
- Your formula sheet has

$f(x)$	$\int f(x)\,dx$
$\sin ax$	$-\frac{1}{a}\cos ax + C$

- With $a = 1$ you get $\int \sin x\,dx = -\cos x + C$.

Integration
- Notice for $\int -\sin 2x\,dx$ the sign changes to positive and you divide by the coefficient 2 to get $\int -\sin 2x\,dx = \frac{\cos 2x}{2} + C$.

Substitution
- Replace x by π and again by $\frac{\pi}{3}$ and subtract.

Area
- Take great care with negatives in this tricky calculation!

HMRN: p. 49

Q5(*a*)

$2y = x-2 \Rightarrow y = \frac{1}{2}x - 1$

$\Rightarrow m = \frac{1}{2}$

gradient of AB is also $\frac{1}{2}$ (parallel)

a point on AB is A(−8, 0). ✓

So equation of AB is

$y - 0 = \frac{1}{2}(x - (-8))$

$\Rightarrow y = \frac{1}{2}(x+8) \Rightarrow 2y = x + 8.$ ✓

To find the points of intersection of the line AB with the circle solve:

$$\left.\begin{aligned} x^2 + y^2 + 6x - 20y - 16 &= 0 \\ 2y &= x + 8 \end{aligned}\right\}$$

Substitute $x = 2y - 8$ in the circle equation:

$(2y - 8)^2 + y^2 + 6(2y - 8) - 20y - 16 = 0$ ✓

$\Rightarrow 4y^2 - 32y + 64 + y^2 + 12y - 48 - 20y - 16 = 0$ ✓

$\Rightarrow 5y^2 - 40y = 0$

$\Rightarrow 5y(y - 8) = 0$

$\Rightarrow y = 0$ or $y = 8$

If $y = 0$ then the point of intersection is point A.

If $y = 8$ then $x = 2 \times 8 - 8 = 8$ and so B is the point (8, 8). ✓

5 marks

Strategy

- To find the points of intersection of the line with the circle their two equations should be solved simultaneously. The circle equation is known, however the equation of the line AB is not known and will need to be found.

Line equation

- The equation of a line passing through (a, b) with gradient m is given by:

$$y - b = m(x - a)$$

- In the case of line AB a point on the line is known, namely A(−8, 0). It has the same gradient as the tangent line since parallel lines have equal gradients.
- The equation of the tangent line needs first to be changed to the form $y = mx + c$ so that m can be determined.

Substitution

- The circle equation is complicated so use the line equation to find x or y in terms of the other variable (letter) and then substitute this expression in the circle equation.
- There are two rearrangements of the line equation: $y = \frac{1}{2}x + 4$ or $x = 2y - 8$. This latter form is better as it avoids the use of fractions.
- In the circle equation every occurrence of x is replaced by $2y - 8$.

Standard form

- After simplifying you should recognise that you are dealing with a quadratic equation. To solve this it needs to be rearranged into "standard form":

$$ay^2 + by + c = 0.$$

In this case $a = 5$, $b = -40$ and $c = 0$.

Coordinates

- You need to identify points A and B with the two values $y = 0$ (for A) and $y = 8$ (for the point B).
- Always use the simpler line equation, not the circle equation, to calculate the other coordinate (in this case $x = 8$).

HMRN: p. 40

Q5(*b*)(i)

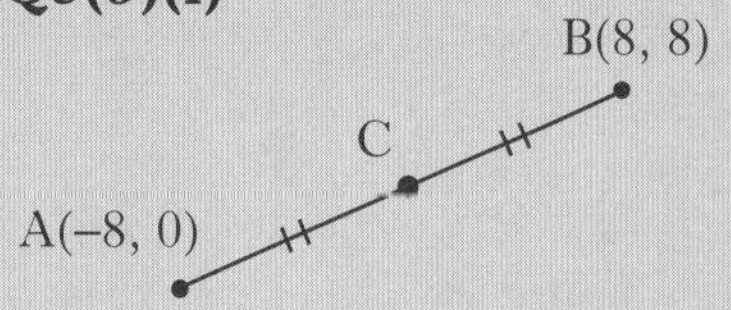

The centre of the circle is the midpoint of AB:

$C\left(\frac{-8+8}{2},\frac{0+8}{2}\right)=C(0,4).$ ✓

The radius is AC

so $AC=\sqrt{(-8-0)^2+(0-4)^2}$

$=\sqrt{64+16}=\sqrt{80}.$ ✓

The centre is C(0, 4) and the radius is $\sqrt{80}$ so the equation of the circle is:

$(x-0)^2+(y-4)^2=(\sqrt{80})^2$

$\Rightarrow x^2+(y-4)^2=80$ ✓

3 marks

Centre

- The centre of a circle lies at the midpoint of any diameter of the circle.
- The result used here is the midpoint formula: the midpoint of AB where $A(x_1, y_1)$ and $B(x_2, y_2)$ is $\left(\frac{x_1+x_2}{2},\frac{y_1+y_2}{2}\right)$. The x-coordinate is the average (mean) of the two x-coordinates. Similarly for the y-coordinate.

Radius

- Alternatively AC^2 could be found using $(-8-0)^2+(0-4)^2$ (no square root sign).
- The result used here is the distance formula: the distance PQ where $P(x_1, y_1)$ and $Q(x_2, y_2)$ is $\sqrt{(x_2-x_1)^2+(y_2-y_1)^2}$
- Squaring −8 and −4 gives positive answers, 64 and 16.
- There is no need to simplify $\sqrt{80}$ as this will be squared in the equation (to give 80).

Equation

- The result used is: The equation of a circle with centre (a, b) and radius r is $(x-a)^2+(y-b)^2=r^2$.
- This result is given on your formulae sheet in the exam (whereas the midpoint formula and the distance formula are not given to you).
- It is not necessary to expand the equation (to get $x^2+y^2-8y-64=0$) for you to gain this mark.

HMRN: p. 7, p. 39

Q5(*b*)(ii)

For the x-axis intercepts set $y=0$ in the equation $x^2+(y-4)^2=80$

$\Rightarrow x^2+(0-4)^2=80$ ✓

$\Rightarrow x^2+16=80 \Rightarrow x^2=64$

$\Rightarrow x=\pm\sqrt{64} \Rightarrow x=\pm 8$

The points of intersection are (−8, 0) and (8, 0) a distance of 16 units. ✓

2 marks

Strategy

- All points on the x-axis have a y-coordinate of zero. This is why substituting $y=0$ in the circle equation produces those points on the circle that are also on the x-axis.

Calculation

- Producing (−8, 0) and (8, 0) will not gain this mark. The question asks for the length of the line joining these two points, i.e. the length of the chord.

HMRN: p. 39

Q6(*a*)

$$\frac{2x^2 - 7x + 6}{x^2 - 4} \quad ✓$$

$$= \frac{(2x-3)(x-2)}{(x-2)(x+2)} = \frac{2x-3}{x+2} \quad ✓$$

2 marks

Factorisation
- Compare a numerical example:
  $\frac{36}{32} = \frac{4 \times 9}{4 \times 8} = \frac{9}{8}$ where the factor 4 is cancelled as it appears both on the top and bottom of the fraction. In the example in the paper, the factor $x - 2$ is cancelled as it similarly appears on the top and bottom of the fraction.

Result
- No further cancelling is possible.

Q6(*b*)

$$\log_3(2x^2 - 7x + 6) - \log_3(x^2 - 4) = 2$$

$$\Rightarrow \log_3\left(\frac{2x^2 - 7x + 6}{x^2 - 4}\right) = 2$$

$$\Rightarrow \log_3\left(\frac{2x-3}{x+2}\right) = 2 \quad ✓$$

$$\Rightarrow \frac{2x-3}{x+2} = 3^2 \quad ✓$$

$$\Rightarrow 2x - 3 = 9(x+2)$$

$$\Rightarrow 2x - 3 = 9x + 18$$

$$\Rightarrow -3 - 18 = 9x - 2x$$

$$\Rightarrow -21 = 7x$$

$$\Rightarrow x = \frac{-21}{7} = -3 \quad ✓$$

3 marks

Use laws of logs
- The law used here is:
  $\log_b m - \log_b n = \log_b \frac{m}{n}$.

Exponential form
- There are two equivalent forms

  $\log_b a = c \longleftrightarrow a = b^c$

  (log form) (exponential form)
- Notice that part (*a*) of your answer is used to replace $\frac{2x^2 - 7x + 6}{x^2 - 4}$ by $\frac{2x-3}{x+2}$
- You cannot use your calculator [log] or [ln] as neither give logs to the base 3.

Solve equation
- At line 4, multiply both sides of the equation by $x + 2$ to get rid of the fraction.
- This is a "linear" equation (there is no x^2 term, only x terms and constants).

HMRN: p. 50

Q7(*a*)

$A = A_0\, e^{-kt}$

when $t = 500$, $A = 0{\cdot}804\, A_0$

So $0{\cdot}804\, A_0 = A_0 e^{-k \times 500}$

$\Rightarrow 0{\cdot}804 = e^{-500k}$ ✓

$\Rightarrow \log_e 0{\cdot}804 = -500k$ ✓

$\Rightarrow k = \frac{\log_e 0{\cdot}804}{-500} = 0{\cdot}0004363\ldots$

So $k \doteq 0{\cdot}000436$ ✓

(to 3 significant figures)

3 marks

Interpretation and substitution
- It is useful to label the equation:

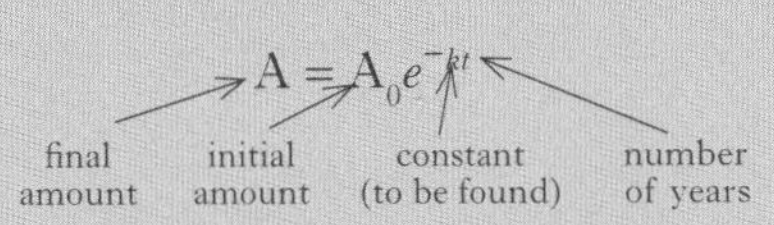

- Notice that to find 80·4% of something, since this is $\frac{80{\cdot}4}{100}$ (0·804), the multiplying factor is 0·804.

Log form
- Here you use $a = b^c \longleftrightarrow \log_b a = c$.

Calculation
- Use [ln] on your calculator. This is the key that gives logs to the base e ($\log_e$).

Q7(b)

So $A = A_0 e^{-0{\cdot}000436t}$

The half-life is the value of t that gives $A = \frac{1}{2}A_0$

$\Rightarrow \frac{1}{2}A_0 = A_0 e^{-0{\cdot}000436t}$

$\Rightarrow \frac{1}{2} = e^{-0{\cdot}000436t}$ ✓

$\Rightarrow \log_e\left(\frac{1}{2}\right) = -0{\cdot}000436t$

$\Rightarrow t = \dfrac{\log_e\left(\frac{1}{2}\right)}{-0{\cdot}0004363\ldots}$

$\Rightarrow t = 1588{\cdot}6\ldots$

The half-life is approximately 1590 years to the nearest 10 years. ✓

2 marks

Substitution

- Since the constant k has been calculated in part (*a*) k can now be replaced in the equation by its value $-0{\cdot}000436$.
- The initial amount is A_0 so $\frac{1}{2}A_0$ is one half of the initial amount. So the final amount A in the equation is replaced by $\frac{1}{2}A_0$ so that the length of time, t, for this reduced amount to remain can then be calculated.
- Notice both sides of the equation have a factor of A_0. Dividing each side by this factor A_0 reduces the equation to the form $a = b^c$.

Log form and Calculation

- Again, as in part (*a*) you have to rearrange the exponential form $a = b^c$ into the logarithmic form $\log_b a = c$.
- Careful with the calculation $\log_e\left(\frac{1}{2}\right)$.

  either use [ln] [0] [·] [5] or

  [ln] [(] [1] [÷] [2] [)] but not

  [ln] [1] [÷] [2]
- Any correct approximation will gain this mark.
- In the calculation, for accuracy, the non-rounded value $-0{\cdot}0004363\ \ldots$ was used.

HMRN: p. 51

Q8(a)

$\boldsymbol{a}.\boldsymbol{b} = |\boldsymbol{a}||\boldsymbol{b}|\cos\theta$

where $\theta = \frac{\pi}{4}$

and $|\boldsymbol{a}| = |\boldsymbol{b}| = 1$ ✓

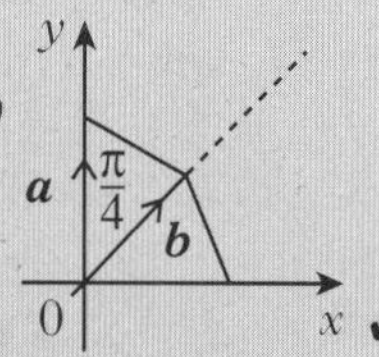

so $\boldsymbol{a}.\boldsymbol{b} = 1 \times 1 \times \cos\frac{\pi}{4} = \frac{1}{\sqrt{2}}$ ✓

2 marks

Scalar product

- Your formulae sheet during the exam gives: $\boldsymbol{a} \cdot \boldsymbol{b} = |\boldsymbol{a}||\boldsymbol{b}|\cos\theta$ where θ is the angle between $\boldsymbol{a}$ and $\boldsymbol{b}$.
- The symmetry of the octagon leads to the angle between $\boldsymbol{a}$ and $\boldsymbol{b}$ of one half of $\frac{\pi}{2}$.
- The term 'unit vector' means a magnitude of 1 unit leading to $|\boldsymbol{a}| = 1$ and $|\boldsymbol{b}| = 1$.

Exact value

- Use the diagram shown and SOHCAHTOA to calculate $\cos\frac{\pi}{4}$.

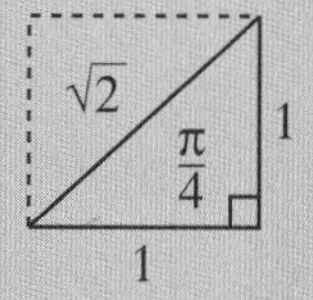

HMRN: p. 46

Q8(b)

$\boldsymbol{p}.\boldsymbol{p} = |\boldsymbol{p}| \times |\boldsymbol{p}| \times \cos 0$ ✓

$= |\boldsymbol{p}|^2 \times 1$

$= |\boldsymbol{p}|^2$ ✓

2 marks

Scalar product

- The angle between $\boldsymbol{p}$ and itself is 0 radians!

Proof

- You should indicate clearly that you know cos0 = 1. You will not gain this mark if "×1" is missing.

HMRN: p. 47

Q8(*c*)

So $|\boldsymbol{p}|^2 = \boldsymbol{p}.\boldsymbol{p}$

$= (\boldsymbol{b}-\boldsymbol{a}).(\boldsymbol{b}-\boldsymbol{a})$ ✓

$= \boldsymbol{b}.\boldsymbol{b} - \boldsymbol{a}.\boldsymbol{b} - \boldsymbol{b}.\boldsymbol{a} + \boldsymbol{a}.\boldsymbol{a}$ ✓

$= |\boldsymbol{b}||\boldsymbol{b}|\cos 0 - \frac{1}{\sqrt{2}} - \frac{1}{\sqrt{2}} + |\boldsymbol{a}||\boldsymbol{a}|\cos 0$

$= 1 - \frac{1}{\sqrt{2}} - \frac{1}{\sqrt{2}} + 1$ ✓

$= 2 - \frac{2}{\sqrt{2}} = 2 - \frac{2\sqrt{2}}{2}$ ✓

$= 2 - \sqrt{2}$ ✓

So $|\boldsymbol{p}|^2 = 2 - \sqrt{2}$

$\Rightarrow |\boldsymbol{p}| = \sqrt{2-\sqrt{2}} = \text{AB}$

So the sides of the octagon have length $\sqrt{2-\sqrt{2}}$ units. ✓

6 marks

Strategy

- Substituting $\boldsymbol{b}-\boldsymbol{a}$ for $\boldsymbol{p}$ in the right-hand side of the result $|\boldsymbol{p}|^2 = \boldsymbol{p}.\boldsymbol{p}$ will then produce $\boldsymbol{a}.\boldsymbol{b}$ terms when the expression is expanded with no brackets.

Expansion

- In some respects the 'dot product' behaves like multiplication of numbers. The expression $(\boldsymbol{b}-\boldsymbol{a}).(\boldsymbol{b}-\boldsymbol{a})$ can be expanded as if you were dealing with an algebraic expression like $(\boldsymbol{b}-\boldsymbol{a})(\boldsymbol{b}-\boldsymbol{a})$. However $\boldsymbol{b}^2$ is not used with vectors, so $\boldsymbol{b}.\boldsymbol{b}$ is used, not $\boldsymbol{b}^2$.

Note also that $\boldsymbol{a}.\boldsymbol{b}$ and $\boldsymbol{b}.\boldsymbol{a}$ are equal.

Substitution

- The result $\boldsymbol{a}.\boldsymbol{b} = \frac{1}{\sqrt{2}}$ is used from part (*a*) with $\boldsymbol{b}.\boldsymbol{a}$ being the same value.

Scalar Product

- This mark is for $|\boldsymbol{b}||\boldsymbol{b}|\cos 0$ and $|\boldsymbol{a}||\boldsymbol{a}|\cos 0$ both having the value 1.

Simplification

- Notice: $\frac{2}{\sqrt{2}} = \frac{2\times\sqrt{2}}{\sqrt{2}\times\sqrt{2}} = \frac{2\sqrt{2}}{2} = \sqrt{2}$.

Proof

- You should state clearly that $|\boldsymbol{p}|$ is the required side of the octagon.
- Take the square root of both sides of the equation $|\boldsymbol{p}|^2 = 2-\sqrt{2}$ to give the final result.

HMRN: p. 47

Q1

$g(f(x))$
$= g(2x^2)$
$=3 - 2x^2$

Choice A.

2 marks

- Always work from the "inside" out in these examples. The "inside" is $f(x)$ and since $f(x) = 2x^2$ you first replace $f(x)$ by $2x^2$.
- Since $g(x) = 3 - x$ the "pattern" is:

  $g(\square) = 3 - \square$

  In this case $2x^2$ is placed in the box.

HMRN: p. 10

Q2

For line L:
$3y - x = 4$
$\Rightarrow 3y = x + 4$
$\Rightarrow y = \frac{1}{3}x + \frac{4}{3}$
So $m_L = \frac{1}{3}$
For line M: $y + 3x = 5$ ✓
$\Rightarrow y = -3x + 5$
So $m_M = -3$
Since $m_L \times m_M = \frac{1}{3} \times (-3) = -1$
The lines are perpendicular
Choice C.

2 marks

- The main results are as follows:

  If two lines have gradients m_1 and m_2 then $m_1 = m_2$ means they are parallel and $m_1 \times m_2 = -1$ means they are perpendicular.
- Remember also that rearranging the equation of a line into the form

  $$y = mx + c$$

  allows you to read off the gradient m.

HMRN: p. 4–5

Q3

$x^2 + y^2 = 6x - 4y - 9$
$\Rightarrow x^2 + y^2 - 6x + 4y + 9 = 0$
The centre is $(3, -2)$
radius $= \sqrt{3^2 + (-2)^2 - 9}$
$= \sqrt{9 + 4 - 9}$
$= \sqrt{4} = 2$ ✓
Choice A.

2 marks

- There is an easy process leading from the circle equation to the centre and then to the radius:

  $$x^2 + y^2 + ax + by + c = 0$$

  Centre: $\left(-\frac{a}{2}, -\frac{b}{2}\right)$

  radius $= \sqrt{\left(-\frac{a}{2}\right)^2 + \left(-\frac{b}{2}\right)^2 - c}$

  In the question you have:

  -6 and 4 leads to $(3, -2)$

  leading to $\sqrt{3^2 + (-2)^2 - 9}$.
- Be very careful the equation is in the form $x^2 + y^2 + ax + by + c = 0$. In this case the 3 terms on the right-hand side of the equation have to be removed to get "= 0" before the above process starts.

HMRN: p. 39

Q4

Let A(2, −3) and B(−4, 1).
Then
$AB = \sqrt{(2-(-4))^2 + (-3-1)^2}$
$= \sqrt{6^2 + (-4)^2}$
$= \sqrt{36 + 16} = \sqrt{52}$
$= \sqrt{4 \times 13} = 2\sqrt{13}$ ✓
Choice D.

2 marks

- The result used here is the distance formula:

  If $A(x_1, y_1)$ and $B(x_2, y_2)$ then

  $AB = \sqrt{(x_2 - x_1)^2 + (y_2 - y_1)^2}$

  This formula is not given to you in the exam.
- When simplifying surds look for square factors, e.g. 4, 9, 16, 25 etc. (in this case 4).

HMRN: p. 7

Q5

$$f(x) = \frac{1}{\sin x} = (\sin x)^{-1}$$

$$\Rightarrow f'(x) = -(\sin x)^{-2} \times \cos x$$

$$= -\frac{1}{(\sin x)^2} \times \cos x$$

$$= -\frac{\cos x}{\sin^2 x}$$

Choice C.

2 marks

- There are two rules used here. One is the index law: $a^{-1} = \frac{1}{a}$. The second is the chain rule for differentiating. Here is the rule in this case:

$$f(x) = (\underset{\substack{\uparrow\\ \sin x}}{g(x)})^{\underset{\substack{\uparrow\\ -1}}{n}} \Rightarrow f'(x) = \underset{\substack{\uparrow\\ -1}}{n}(\underset{\substack{\uparrow\\ \sin x}}{g(x)})^{\underset{\substack{\uparrow\\ -2}}{n-1}} \times \underset{\substack{\uparrow\\ \cos x}}{g'(x)}$$

- Simplifying the result again involves an index law: $a^{-n} = \frac{1}{a^n}$. In this case $a^{-2} = \frac{1}{a^2}$
- Notice that $(\sin x)^2$ and $\sin^2 x$ are identical but that in the 1st form brackets are essential as $\sin x^2$ could mean sine of angle x^2 not $\sin x$ squared.

HMRN: p. 48

Q6

For $y = (2x - 1)^2 - 3$

The minimum value occurs when

$2x - 1 = 0 \Rightarrow x = \frac{1}{2}$

When $x = \frac{1}{2}$ $y = 0^2 - 3 = -3$

So minimum point is $\left(\frac{1}{2}, -3\right)$

Choice D.

2 marks

- Squaring a quantity always results in a positive or a zero value, never a negative value. So the least value that $(2x - 1)^2$ can take is zero. This will occur when zero is squared, i.e. when $2x - 1 = 0$.
- Graphically you have:

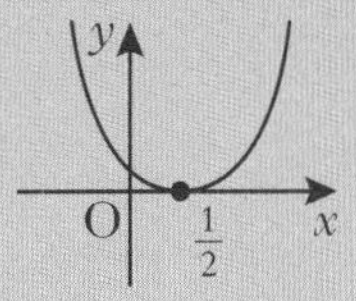

graph of $y = (2x - 1)^2$

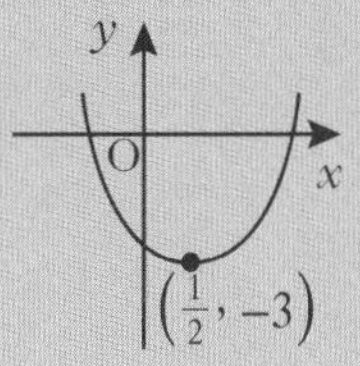

graph of $y = (2x - 1)^2 - 3$

HMRN: p. 14

Q7

At the limit 24: $u_{n+1} = ku_n + 8$ becomes $24 = k \times 24 + 8$

$\Rightarrow 24k = 16 \Rightarrow k = \frac{16}{24} = \frac{2}{3}$

Choice C.

2 marks

- When the limit number is reached then applying the recurrence relation (multiply by k then add 8) to this limit will produce the limit. This is the definition of a limit! So applying the recurrence relation to 24 will produce 24 again, i.e. $24 = k \times 24 + 8$.
- Alternatively for $u_{n+1} = au_n + b$ then $L = \frac{b}{1 - a}$ (provided $-1 < a < 1$) so in this case $L = 24$, $b = 8$ and $a = k$ giving

$$24 = \frac{8}{1 - k} \Rightarrow 24(1 - k) = 8$$

$$\Rightarrow 24 - 24k = 8 \Rightarrow 24k = 16$$

$$\Rightarrow k = \frac{16}{24} = \frac{2}{3}$$

HMRN: p. 24

Q8

$\frac{2}{1-x^2}$ is not defined when

$1 - x^2 = 0$

$\Rightarrow x^2 = 1$

$\Rightarrow x = \pm 1$

Choice D.

2 marks

- The largest domain of a function f is the set of all values that can be "processed" by f. The usual problems that arise in this "processing" are attempting to find the square root of a negative number or attempting to divide by zero. In this case you need to avoid $1 - x^2$ taking the value zero.

HMRN: p. 9

Q9

Let A(−1, 0) and B(5, 8)

The centre is

$$C\left(\frac{-1+5}{2}, \frac{0+8}{2}\right) = C(2,4)$$

Radius = AC

$$= \sqrt{(2-(-1))^2 + (4-0)^2}$$

$$= \sqrt{3^2 + 4^2} = \sqrt{9+16}$$

$$= \sqrt{25} = 5$$

So the equation is

$(x - 2)^2 + (y - 4)^2 = 5^2$

$\Rightarrow (x - 2)^2 + (y - 4)^2 = 25$

Choice A.

2 marks

- The centre of a circle lies at the midpoint of any diameter of the circle. To locate the centre in this case you are using the midpoint result:

  The midpoint of AB where A(x_1, y_1) and B(x_2, y_2) is $\left(\frac{x_1+x_2}{2}, \frac{y_1+y_2}{2}\right)$.
- You are also using the distance formula:

  $AB = \sqrt{(x_2-x_1)^2 + (y_2-y_1)^2}$ to find the length of the radius.
- The equation of the circle with centre (a, b) and radius r is $(x - a)^2 + (y - b)^2 = r^2$. In this case $a = 2$, $b = 4$ and $r = 5$.

HMRN: p. 7, p. 39

Q10

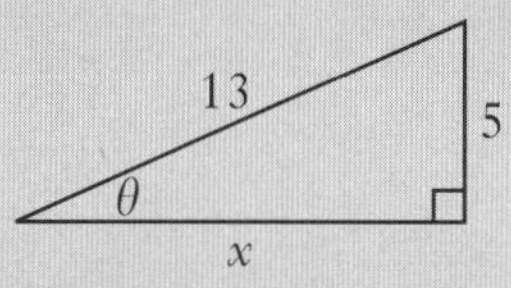

$x^2 = 13^2 - 5^2$

$= 169 - 25$

$= 144$

$\Rightarrow x = \sqrt{144} = 12$

So $\sin\theta = \frac{5}{13}$ and $\cos\theta = \frac{12}{13}$

$\sin 2\theta = 2 \sin\theta \cos\theta$

$$= 2 \times \frac{5}{13} \times \frac{12}{13}$$

$$= \frac{120}{169}$$

Choice D.

2 marks

- You may well know that a triangle with sides 5, 12 and 13 is a right-angled triangle, and so you were able to write down 12 with no calculation.
- It is surprising the number of mistakes that arise from using 'SOHCAHTOA' wrongly. Sometimes it is the 'naming' of the sides that goes wrong.

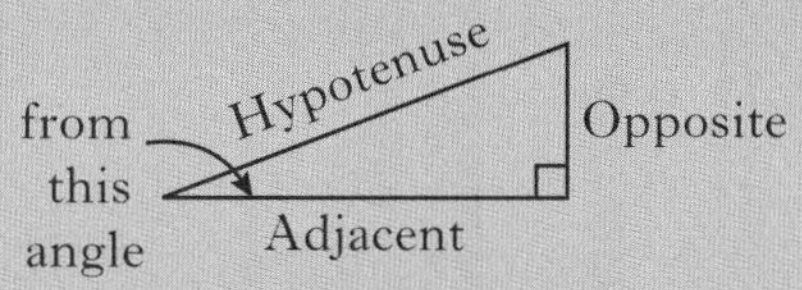

- The formula sin2A = 2sinAcosA is given to you on your formulae sheet during the exam, but nevertheless you should learn this formula along with the other double angle formulae.

HMRN: p. 35–36

Q11

$\cos 2a° = 2\cos^2 a° - 1$

$$= 2 \times \left(\frac{e}{d}\right)^2 - 1$$

$$= \frac{2e^2}{d^2} - 1$$

$$= \frac{2e^2}{d^2} - \frac{d^2}{d^2}$$

$$= \frac{2e^2 - d^2}{d^2}$$

Choice B.

2 marks

- There are three versions of $\cos 2a°$: $2\cos^2 a° - 1$, $\cos^2 a° - \sin^2 a°$ and $1 - 2\sin^2 a°$.

  The form $2\cos^2 a° - 1$ leads directly to the correct choice, the others do not.

  For example:

  $\cos^2 a° - \sin^2 a°$

  $= \left(\frac{e}{d}\right)^2 - \left(\frac{f}{d}\right)^2 = \frac{e^2}{d^2} - \frac{f^2}{d^2}$

  $= \frac{e^2 - f^2}{d^2}$

  Now use Pythagoras' Theorem

  At this stage replace f^2 by $d^2 - e^2$ to give

  $\frac{e^2 - (d^2 - e^2)}{d^2} = \frac{e^2 - d^2 + e^2}{d^2} = \frac{2e^2 - d^2}{d^2}$.

HMRN: p. 35

Q12

$\int (3-2x)^4\,dx$

$= \dfrac{(3-2x)^5}{-2\times 5} + C$

$= -\dfrac{1}{10}(3-2x)^5 + C$

Choice A.

2 marks

- Here you are using the "special integral" result:

  $\int (ax+b)^n\,dx = \dfrac{(ax+b)^{n+1}}{a(n+1)} + C$

  in this case with $a=-2$, $b=3$ and $n=4$. So take care to include the extra factor a, in this case -2. This is the coefficient of x in the term $3-2x$ and should appear on the bottom of the fraction.

- Either $-\dfrac{(3-2x)^5}{10}$ or $-\dfrac{1}{10}(3-2x)^5$ is acceptable but not $\dfrac{(3-2x)^5}{-10}$ if this were a written question in Paper 2 for instance.

HMRN: p. 49

Q13

The four areas I, II, III and IV shown in the diagram are all equal due to the symmetry of the graphs.

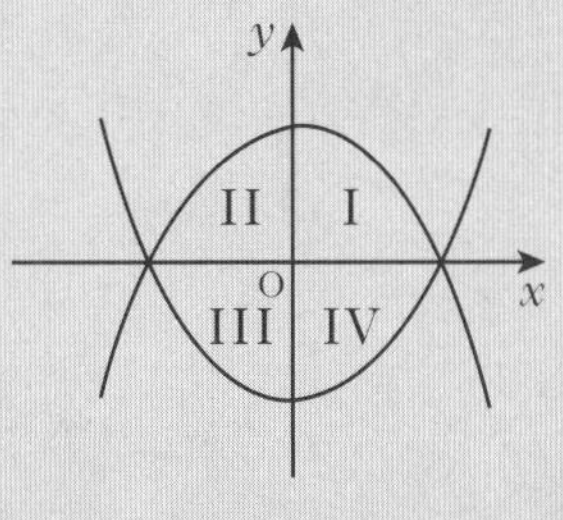

You need to identify which choice is **not** Area I + Area IV.

Choice A: $\int_0^2 (4-x^2)\,dx$ gives area I

so $2\int_0^2 (4-x^2)\,dx$ gives 2 × area I

= area I + area IV

Choice B: $\int_{-2}^2 (4-x^2)\,dx$ gives

area I + area II

= area I + area IV

Choice C: Since Area IV is located below the x-axis this means that $\int_0^2 (4-x^2)\,dx$ gives the negative of area IV so

$-\int_0^2 (x^2-4)\,dx$ gives area IV and so

$\int_0^2 (4-x^2)\,dx - \int_0^2 (x^2-4)\,dx$ gives area I + area IV

So choice D is the right answer. (It gives area I − area IV).

2 marks

- Here are the essential results for this question:

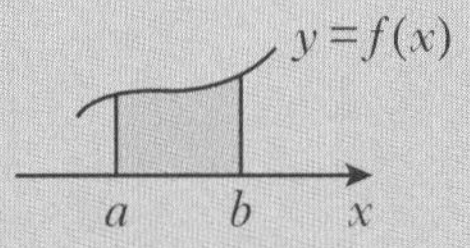

The shaded area is given by $\int_a^b f(x)\,dx$

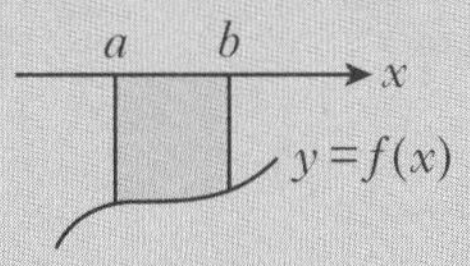

The shaded area is given by $-\int_a^b f(x)\,dx$

The main idea being that areas below the x-axis will be given a negative sign by the integral so you must cancel this by attaching a negative sign (the negative of a negative makes a positive – and all areas should be positive!)

- The best strategy in a case like this where the choices are fairly complicated is to tackle each choice and determine whether it is correct or not. If you establish one choice as correct make sure you double-check by working through all the other choices too.
- Mistakes are also made by muddling the two curves. The top curve is $y = 4 - x^2$ and the bottom curve is $y = x^2 - 4$.

HMRN: p. 32

Q14

The graph $y = \log_5 2x$ can be obtained from the graph $y = \log_5 x$ by an x-axis scaling with scale factor $\frac{1}{2}$

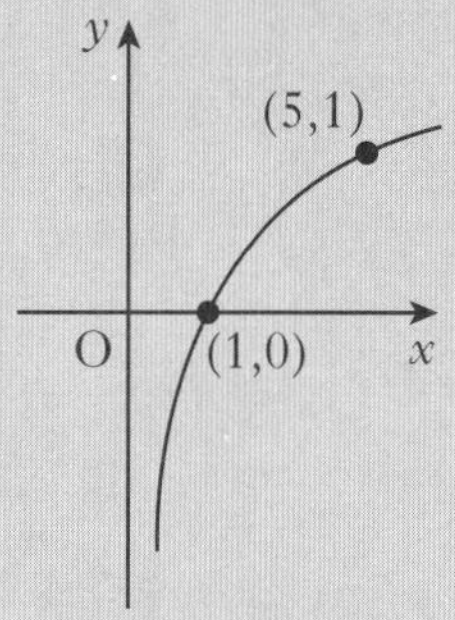

this graph is $y = \log_5 x$

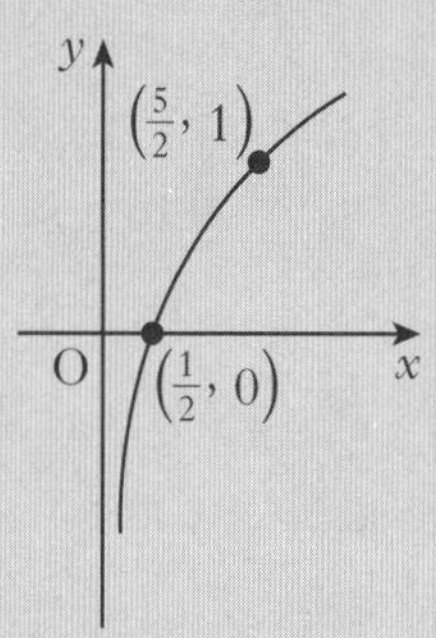

this graph is $y = \log_5 2x$

Choice B.

2 marks

- It is possible to work through the choices in the following manner:

  Choice A has two points on the graph, namely $\left(\frac{1}{2}, 0\right)$ and (5,1). If a point lies on a graph then its coordinates satisfy the equation of the graph. So for $\left(\frac{1}{2}, 0\right)$ $x = \frac{1}{2}$ and $y = 0$. Substituting these values into the equation $y = \log_5 2x$ you get $0 = \log_5 1$ giving $5^0 = 1$ which is true. For point (5,1) $x = 5$ and $y = 1$ giving $1 = \log_5 10 \Rightarrow 5^1 = 10$ which is not true. The point does not lie on the curve, so choice A is not correct. The other choices can be worked through in a similar manner.

HMRN: p. 13, p. 51

Q15

Method 1

$$\log_3\left(\frac{1}{3}\right) = \log_3\left(3^{-1}\right)$$
$$= -\log_3 3 = -1$$

Method 2

$$\log_3\left(\frac{1}{3}\right) = \log_3 1 - \log_3 3$$
$$= 0 - 1 = -1$$

Method 3

$$x = \log_3\left(\frac{1}{3}\right) \Rightarrow 3^x = \frac{1}{3}$$
$$\Rightarrow x = -1 \left(\text{as } 3^{-1} = \frac{1}{3}\right)$$

Choice A.

2 marks

- The various log laws used here are:

  Method 1 $\quad \log_b a^n = n\log_b a$

  $\log_b b = 1$

  Method 2 $\quad \log_b\left(\frac{m}{n}\right) = \log_b m - \log_b n$

  $\log_b 1 = 0$

  Method 3 $\quad c = \log_b a \Rightarrow b^c = a$

- It is possible to read $\log_b a$ as: "what power do you raise b to, to get a?" e.g. $\log_3 9$ becomes "what power do you raise 3 to, to get 9?". The answer to this is 2 (since $3^2 = 9$). So $\log_3\left(\frac{1}{3}\right)$ becomes "what power do you raise 3 to, to get $\frac{1}{3}$?" The answer to this is -1 (since $3^{-1} = \frac{1}{3}$).

HMRN: p. 50

Q16

$$\begin{pmatrix} m \\ 1 \\ -1 \end{pmatrix} . \begin{pmatrix} 1 \\ 2 \\ -1 \end{pmatrix} = 0$$

$\Rightarrow m \times 1 + 1 \times 2 + (-1) \times (-1) = 0$

$\Rightarrow m + 2 + 1 = 0$

$\Rightarrow m + 3 = 0$

$\Rightarrow m = -3$

Choice A.

2 marks

- The scalar or dot product of two perpendicular vectors is zero, i.e. if $\boldsymbol{v}$ and $\boldsymbol{w}$ are perpendicular then $\boldsymbol{v.w} = 0$. This is the result used in this question.

- If $\boldsymbol{v} = \begin{pmatrix} x_1 \\ y_1 \\ z_1 \end{pmatrix}$ and $\boldsymbol{w} = \begin{pmatrix} x_2 \\ y_2 \\ z_2 \end{pmatrix}$ then

  $\boldsymbol{v.w} = x_1x_2 + y_1y_2 + z_1z_2$

HMRN: p. 46

Q17

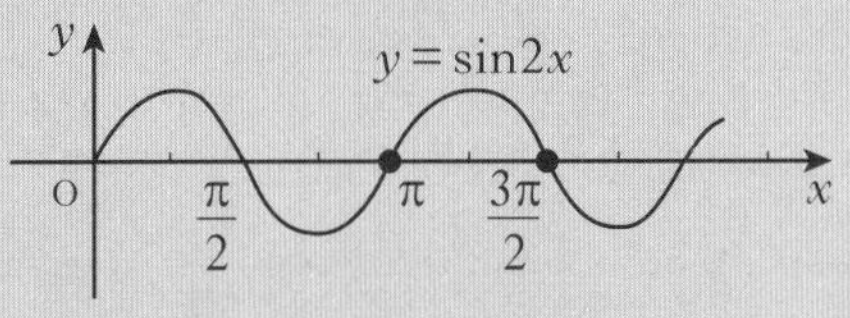

In the range $\frac{\pi}{2} < x \leq \frac{3\pi}{2}$

$\sin 2x = 0$ for only two values of x, namely $x = \pi$ and $x = \frac{3\pi}{2}$

Choice C.

2 marks

- The graph $y = \sin 2x$ has 2 cycles from 0 to 2π where $y = \sin x$ only has one.
- You should always pay close attention to the inequality signs. In this case suppose the range was $\frac{\pi}{2} \leq x \leq \frac{3\pi}{2}$, then Choice B would have been the correct choice as the value $x = \frac{\pi}{2}$ is included. The two signs $\leq$ and $<$ give very different answers.
- An alternative method is to consider solutions to $y = \sin\theta = 0$ giving $\theta = 0, \pi, 2\pi, \ldots$ And replacing θ by $2x$ gives $2x = 0, \pi, 2\pi, 3\pi, 4\pi, \ldots$

  $\Rightarrow x = 0, \frac{\pi}{2}, \pi, \frac{3\pi}{2}, 2\pi, \ldots$
- It is also possible to proceed as follows:

  $\sin 2x = 0 \Rightarrow 2\sin x\cos x = 0$

  $\Rightarrow \sin x = 0$ or $\cos x = 0$

  $\Rightarrow x = 0, \pi, 2\pi, \ldots$ or $x = \frac{\pi}{2}, \frac{3\pi}{2}, \ldots$

  Combining these solutions since they are all valid possibilities gives:

  $\Rightarrow x = 0, \frac{\pi}{2}, \pi, \frac{3\pi}{2}, 2\pi$, etc.

  (In both methods above you then need to impose the condition $\frac{\pi}{2} < x \leq \frac{3\pi}{2}$ leading to Choice C).

HMRN: p. 16–17

Q18

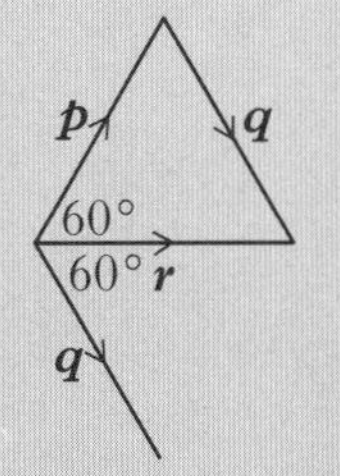

Unit vectors means:
$|\boldsymbol{p}| = |\boldsymbol{q}| = |\boldsymbol{r}| = 1$

$\boldsymbol{p}.(\boldsymbol{q}+\boldsymbol{r}) = \boldsymbol{p}.\boldsymbol{q} + \boldsymbol{p}.\boldsymbol{r}$

$= |\boldsymbol{p}||\boldsymbol{q}|\cos 120° + |\boldsymbol{p}||\boldsymbol{r}|\cos 60°$

$= 1 \times 1 \times \left(-\frac{1}{2}\right) + 1 \times 1 \times \frac{1}{2}$

$= -\frac{1}{2} + \frac{1}{2} = 0$

So I is correct

$\boldsymbol{p}.(\boldsymbol{q}-\boldsymbol{r}) = \boldsymbol{p}.\boldsymbol{q} - \boldsymbol{p}.\boldsymbol{r}$

$= -\frac{1}{2} - \frac{1}{2} = -1$

(from above)

So II is not correct

Choice B.

2 marks

- Recall that a unit vector has magnitude of 1 unit. In this case this leads to:

  $|\boldsymbol{p}| = 1$, $|\boldsymbol{q}| = 1$ and $\boldsymbol{r} = |1$
- For calculation $\boldsymbol{p}.\boldsymbol{q}$ you have to make sure $\boldsymbol{p}$ and $\boldsymbol{q}$ come out from the same point. The angle between $\boldsymbol{p}$ and $\boldsymbol{q}$ is not 60° as you may think from:

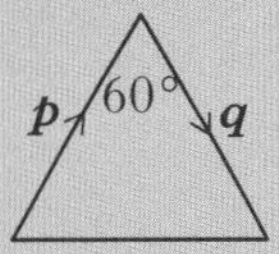

$\boldsymbol{p}$ is going "in" to the vertex and $\boldsymbol{q}$ is coming "out" of the vertex. The diagram in the solution shows another line representing $\boldsymbol{q}$ showing that 120° (60° + 60°) is the angle.

HMRN: p. 47

Q19

$2\cos^2 x = 1 \Rightarrow \cos^2 x = \frac{1}{2}$

$\Rightarrow \cos x = \pm\sqrt{\frac{1}{2}} \Rightarrow \cos x = \pm\frac{1}{\sqrt{2}}$

x could be in all four quadrants

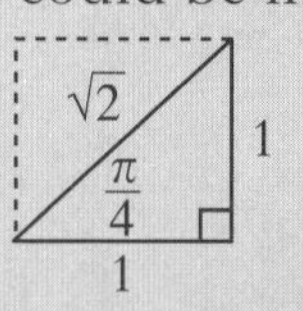

The 1st quadrant angle is $\frac{\pi}{4}$

So

$$x = \frac{\pi}{4} \text{ or } \pi - \frac{\pi}{4} \text{ or } \pi + \frac{\pi}{4} \text{ or } 2\pi - \frac{\pi}{4}$$

$$\Rightarrow x = \frac{\pi}{4} \text{ or } \frac{3\pi}{4} \text{ or } \frac{5\pi}{4} \text{ or } \frac{7\pi}{4}$$

Choice C.

2 marks

- You should be careful when solving equations and you take the square root of each side (to get rid of a squared term) to introduce the ± sign. This allows for both positive and negative values.
- You should recognise $\frac{1}{\sqrt{2}}$ as an exact value for $\cos x$ leading to $\frac{\pi}{4}$ as shown.
- You have no calculator available for paper 1 questions and so no access to the $\boxed{\cos^{-1}}$ button!
- You may have been taught:

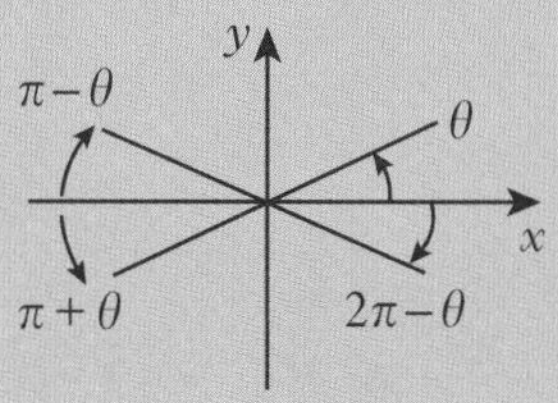

Where θ is the 1st quadrant angle.

In this case $\frac{\pi}{4}$

- Calculations using radians can be easier thinking like this:

$\pi + \frac{\pi}{4} = \frac{4\pi}{4} + \frac{\pi}{4} = \frac{4\pi + \pi}{4} = \frac{5\pi}{4}$

π is 4 lots of $\frac{\pi}{4}$. Add this to 1 lot of $\frac{\pi}{4}$ resulting in 5 lots of $\frac{\pi}{4}$.

Similarly

$2\pi - \frac{\pi}{4} = \frac{8\pi}{4} - \frac{\pi}{4} = \frac{8\pi - \pi}{4} = \frac{7\pi}{4}$

2π is 8 lots of $\frac{\pi}{4}$, take away 1 lot of $\frac{\pi}{4}$ results in 7 lots of $\frac{\pi}{4}$.

HMRN: p. 34

Q20

Consider Choice A:

$p^{(q^p)} = q \Rightarrow \log_e p^{(q^p)} = \log_e q$

$\Rightarrow q^p \log_e p = \log_e q$

$\Rightarrow q^p = \frac{\log_e q}{\log_e p}$

so Choice A is equal to q^p.

Now consider Choice C:

changing $p^{(q^p)} = q$ to logarithmic form gives $\log_p q = q^p$

so Choice C is equal to q^p.

Finally consider Choice D:

$p^{(q^p)} = q$

$\Rightarrow \log_q p^{(q^p)} = \log_q q$

$\Rightarrow q^p \log_q p = 1$

$\Rightarrow q^p = \frac{1}{\log_q p}$

so Choice D also equals q^p.

This leaves: Choice B.

2 marks

- There are several strategies being used here to determine the correct choice. For Choice A you are taking log to the base e of both sides of the equation and for Choice D you are taking log to the base q of both sides. In both cases you then use the result $\log_b a^n = n\log_b a$ which brings the power q^p down to the front of the expression.

For Choice C you are using the equivalent logarithmic form:

$$b^a = c \Rightarrow \log_b c = a$$

HMRN: p. 50

Q21

$m_{AB} = \tan\theta = \sqrt{2}$. ✓

A point on AB is A $(-1, 0)$ ✓

so the equation of AB is:

$$y - 0 = \sqrt{2}\,(x+1) \quad ✓$$

$$\Rightarrow \quad y = \sqrt{2}x + \sqrt{2}$$

3 marks

Strategy

- You are using $y - b = m(x - a)$ and so need to determine the gradient.

Gradient

- This mark is for identifying $m = \tan\theta$ and therefore using $\sqrt{2}$.

Equation

- For $y - b = m(x - a)$ using $(-1, 0)$ gives $a = -1$ and $b = 0$. Also $m = \sqrt{2}$.
- Simplification is not necessary to gain this mark.
- Don't be put off by the fact that there is a surd $(\sqrt{2})$ in the equation. This is not usual but certainly not wrong!

HMRN: p. 4–6

Q22(*a*)

$$u_{n+1} = \frac{1}{k}u_n + 1$$

$$u_1 = \frac{1}{k}u_0 + 1$$

$$= \frac{1}{k} \times k^2 + 1$$

$$= k + 1 \quad ✓$$

$$u_2 = \frac{1}{k}u_1 + 1$$

$$= \frac{1}{k}(k+1) + 1$$

$$= 1 + \frac{1}{k} + 1$$

$$= 2 + \frac{1}{k} \quad ✓$$

2 marks

Term u_1

- Here is a useful diagram:

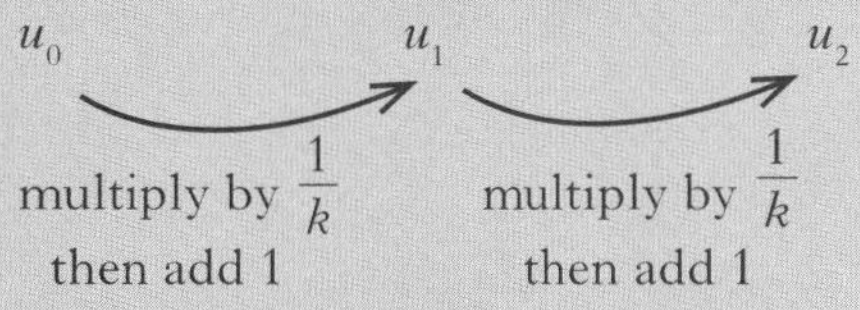

The sequence starts with u_0 which you are told is k^2. So you have:

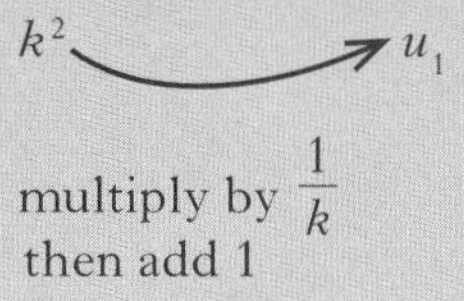

This leads to $\frac{1}{k} \times k^2 + 1$ giving u_1

- Simplification involves $\frac{1}{k} \times k^2$:

$$\frac{1}{k} \times k^2 = \frac{1}{k} \times \frac{k^2}{1} = \frac{k^2}{k} = \frac{k \times \cancel{k}^1}{\cancel{k}^1} = k$$

Notice that the top and bottom of the fraction can be divided by k, i.e. k is cancelled.

Term u_2

- $u_1 = k + 1$ from previous work. Apply the recurrence relation to $k + 1$ then simplify.

HMRN: p. 23

Q22(*b*)

$u_2 = 3k$

and so using the result from (*a*):

$$3k = 2 + \frac{1}{k}$$

$$\Rightarrow 3k^2 = 2k + 1$$

$$\Rightarrow 3k^2 - 2k - 1 = 0 \quad ✓$$

$$\Rightarrow (3k+1)(k-1) = 0$$

$$\Rightarrow 3k + 1 = 0 \text{ or } k - 1 = 0$$

$$k = -\frac{1}{3} \text{ or } k = 1 \quad ✓$$

2 marks

Standard form

- Multiply both sides by k to get rid of the fraction. You then should recognise a quadratic equation and write it in the standard way:

$$ak^2 + bk + c = 0.$$

Solutions

- Factorisation gives solutions $-\frac{1}{3}$ and 1.

Q22(*b*) continued

For the recurrence relation $u_{n+1} = \frac{1}{k}u_n + 1$ the multiplier is $\frac{1}{k}$. When $k = -\frac{1}{3}$

$$\frac{1}{k} = \frac{1}{-\frac{1}{3}} = \frac{1 \times 3}{-\frac{1}{3} \times 3} = \frac{3}{-1} = -3$$

when $k = 1$

$$\frac{1}{k} = \frac{1}{1} = 1$$

For a limit to exist:

$$-1 < \text{multiplier} < 1$$

So there is no limit in either case as -3 and 1 are outside this range. ✓

1 mark

Limit condition

- The result you are using here is:

  a limit exists for the sequence generated by $u_{n+1} = mu_n + c$ whenever $-1 < m < 1$, i.e. the multiplier m lies between -1 and 1. For any value of m outside this range the corresponding sequence will have no limit.

- In this case, i.e $u_{n+1} = \frac{1}{k}u_n + 1$, the multiplier is $\frac{1}{k}$ and so the two values $-\frac{1}{3}$ and 1 are not values of the multiplier, they are only values of k. You have to calculate the value of the multiplier for each of these values of k.
- Note that 1 does not lie in the range "$-1 <$ multiplier < 1". If the multiplier is 1 the resulting sequence has no limit.

Q23(*a*)

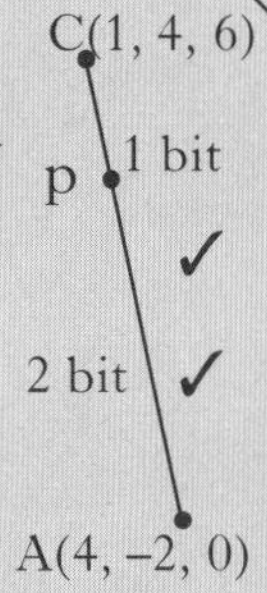

Since AP : PC = 2 : 1

$$\overrightarrow{AP} = 2\overrightarrow{PC}$$ ✓

$$\Rightarrow \boldsymbol{p} - \boldsymbol{a} = 2(\boldsymbol{c} - \boldsymbol{p})$$

$$\Rightarrow \boldsymbol{p} - \boldsymbol{a} = 2\boldsymbol{c} - 2\boldsymbol{p}$$ ✓

$$\Rightarrow \boldsymbol{p} + 2\boldsymbol{p} = 2\boldsymbol{c} + \boldsymbol{a}$$

$$\Rightarrow 3\boldsymbol{p} = 2\boldsymbol{c} + \boldsymbol{a}$$

So

$$3\boldsymbol{p} = 2\begin{pmatrix}1\\4\\6\end{pmatrix} + \begin{pmatrix}4\\-2\\0\end{pmatrix} = \begin{pmatrix}6\\6\\12\end{pmatrix}$$ ✓

$$\Rightarrow \boldsymbol{p} = \frac{1}{3}\begin{pmatrix}6\\6\\12\end{pmatrix} = \begin{pmatrix}2\\2\\4\end{pmatrix}$$

So P (2, 2, 4) ✓

4 marks

Strategy

- Other relationships are possible, e.g. $\overrightarrow{PC} = \frac{1}{3}\overrightarrow{AC}$, $3\overrightarrow{PC} = \overrightarrow{AC}$, $\overrightarrow{PA} = \frac{2}{3}\overrightarrow{CA}$ etc.
- Make sure that the directions of the line segments match, e.g. $\overrightarrow{AP}$ is not twice $\overrightarrow{CP}$ as the directions are opposite.

Position vectors

- The main result used here is $\overrightarrow{AB} = \boldsymbol{b} - \boldsymbol{a}$ where $\boldsymbol{a}$ and $\boldsymbol{b}$ are the position vectors of the points A and B.

Components

- Notice the equation $\boldsymbol{p} - \boldsymbol{a} = 2(\boldsymbol{c} - \boldsymbol{p})$ can be rearranged using your algebra skills. The aim is to make $\boldsymbol{p}$ the subject.

Coordinates

- You have to convert $\boldsymbol{p} = \begin{pmatrix}2\\2\\4\end{pmatrix}$, which are components of a position vector, to P(2, 2, 4), which are coordinates of a point. This final mark is for the coordinates not the components.

HMRN: p. 45

Q23(*b*)

$$\overrightarrow{BP} = \boldsymbol{p} - \boldsymbol{b} = \begin{pmatrix}2\\2\\4\end{pmatrix} - \begin{pmatrix}3\\5\\0\end{pmatrix} = \begin{pmatrix}-1\\-3\\4\end{pmatrix}$$

So $\overrightarrow{BP} = -\boldsymbol{i} - 3\boldsymbol{j} + 4\boldsymbol{k}$ ✓

1 mark

Unit vectors

- The alternative to $\begin{pmatrix}a\\b\\c\end{pmatrix}$ is $a\boldsymbol{i} + b\boldsymbol{j} + c\boldsymbol{k}$.

HMRN: p. 47

Q24

$2(\sqrt{3}\cos x - \sin x) = k\cos(x+a)$

$\Rightarrow 2\sqrt{3}\cos x - 2\sin x$

$= k\cos x\cos a - k\sin x\sin a$ ✓

So $k\cos a = 2\sqrt{3}$, $k\sin a = 2$ } Since cos$a$ and sin$a$ are positive, a is in the 1st quadrant. ✓

$\dfrac{k\sin a}{k\cos a} = \dfrac{2}{2\sqrt{3}}$

$\Rightarrow \dfrac{\sin a}{\cos a} = \dfrac{1}{\sqrt{3}}$

$\Rightarrow \tan a = \dfrac{1}{\sqrt{3}}$

$\Rightarrow a = \dfrac{\pi}{6}$ ✓

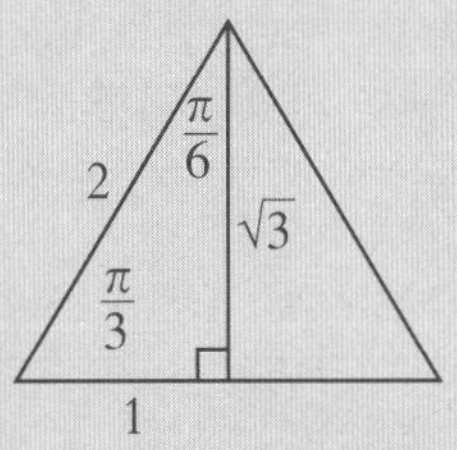

Also

$(k\sin a)^2 + (k\cos a)^2 = 2^2 + (2\sqrt{3})^2$

$\Rightarrow k^2\sin^2 a + k^2\cos^2 a = 4 + 12$

$\Rightarrow k^2(\sin^2 a + \cos^2 a) = 16$

$\Rightarrow k^2 \times 1 = 16 \Rightarrow k^2 = 16$ ✓

$\Rightarrow k = 4\ (k > 0)$

So $2(\sqrt{3}\cos x - \sin x)$

$= 4\cos\left(x + \dfrac{\pi}{6}\right)$

4 marks

Expansion

- You have on your formulae sheet:

  $\cos(A \pm B) = \cos A\cos B \mp \sin A\sin B$.

- This mark is for explicitly writing the expansion: $k\cos x\cos a - k\sin x\sin a$.

Compare coefficients

- cos$x$ is multiplied by $2\sqrt{3}$ (line two) and by $k\cos a$ (line three). These two coefficients are equal, i.e. $k\cos a = 2\sqrt{3}$. Similarly for the coefficients of sin$x$.
- Notice that if both coefficients are negative, e.g. -2 and $-k\sin a$, the negative sign can be ignored.

Find *a*

- You know (from last year) that $\dfrac{\sin a}{\cos a} = \tan a$.
- Be careful of the order in this division. It is not $\dfrac{2\sqrt{3}}{2}$ as this would be $\dfrac{\cos a}{\sin a}$ which is not equal to tan a.
- You should recognise $\dfrac{1}{\sqrt{3}}$ as an exact value for tan a coming from the "half an equilateral triangle" diagram.
- Notice that 30° is not an option. To gain this mark requires radian measure for the angle.

Find *k*

- The result $\sin^2 a + \cos^2 a = 1$ is being used, which is the reason both sides of the equations are squared and then added.
- $k^2 = 16$ normally should lead to $k = 4$ or -4 but in this context k is always positive.

HMRN: p. 53–54

Q25(*a*)

−4	1	4	−25	−100
		−4	0	100
	1	0	−25	0

✓ ✓

So when $x = -4$

$x^3 + 4x^2 - 25x - 100 = 0$

so $x = -4$ is a root of this equation and therefore $x + 4$ is a factor $x^3 + 4x^2 - 25x - 100$ ✓

$= (x + 4)(x^2 - 25)$ ✓

$= (x + 4)(x - 5)(x + 5)$ ✓

5 marks

Strategy

- Use the "synthetic division scheme".

Calculation

- This mark is for the correct entries in the table.

Interpret 0

- A clear statement of what you have found.

Quadratic factor

- For this mark $x + 4$ and $x^2 - 25$ should appear.

Fully factorised

- All three factors multiplied together are required to gain this final mark.

HMRN: p. 25–26

Q25(*b*)

For points of intersection solve:

$$\left.\begin{aligned} y &= x+4 \\ y &= x^3+4x^2-24x-96 \end{aligned}\right\}$$

$\Rightarrow x^3 + 4x^2 - 24x - 96 = x + 4$ ✓

$\Rightarrow x^3 + 4x^2 - 24x - x - 96 - 4 = 0$

$\Rightarrow x^3 + 4x^2 - 25x - 100 = 0$

$\Rightarrow (x + 4)(x - 5)(x + 5) = 0$

$\Rightarrow x = -4$ or $x = 5$ or $x = -5$ ✓

So there are exactly three points of intersection.

2 marks

Strategy

- Your method here is to set the two expressions for y equal to each other and solve the resulting equation. The number of distinct solutions you obtain will be the number of points of intersection.
- The word "hence" implies that you should use the results found in part (*a*).
- "Otherwise" implies there are other approaches than using the results of (*a*). For instance, it is possible to use a Graphics calculator, but to gain full marks sketches and coordinates should be clear. Justification is vital. Normally the advice is – do not read answers from a Graphics calculator – working is essential.

Statement

- A clear statement explaining what you have found is required.

HMRN: p. 26

Q26(*a*)

$x^2 + (y - 5)^2 = r^2$ ✓

1 mark

Equation

- The equation $(x - a)^2 + (y - b)^2 = r^2$ represents a circle with centre (a, b) and radius r. This fact is given on your formulae sheet during the exam.

HMRN: p. 39

Q26(*b*)

Since $y = 15 - 3x$ is a tangent then solving:

$$\left.\begin{aligned} y &= 15-3x \\ x^2+(y-5)^2 &= r^2 \end{aligned}\right\} \text{will give only one solution}$$

$\Rightarrow x^2 + (15 - 3x - 5)^2 = r^2$ ✓

$\Rightarrow x^2 + (10 - 3x)^2 = r^2$

$\Rightarrow x^2 + 100 - 60x + 9x^2 = r^2$

$\Rightarrow 10x^2 - 60x + 100 - r^2 = 0$ ✓

For one solution the Discriminant of this equation is zero. ✓

so $(-60)^2 - 4 \times 10 \times (100 - r^2) = 0$

$\Rightarrow 3600 - 4000 + 40r^2 = 0$ ✓

$\Rightarrow 40r^2 = 400 \Rightarrow r^2 = 10$

So $r = \sqrt{10}$ $(r > 0)$ ✓

5 marks

Strategy

- You are solving the two equations simultaneously and imposing a "one solution only" condition. So this mark is for substitution in the circle equation as a 1st step along the way.

Standard form

- You recognise a quadratic equation and rearrange to the form: $ax^2 + bx + c = 0$.

Discriminant

- To impose the "one solution only" condition involves setting the discriminant to zero.

a*, *b* and *c

- $a = 10$, $b = -60$ and $c = 100 - r^2$ where $b^2 - 4ac$ is the discriminant.

Calculation

- Check from the diagram whether a value of just over $3(\sqrt{10})$ makes sense for the radius, bearing in mind the centre lies 5 units up from the origin.

HMRN: p. 41

Q1(*a*)

$\cos(a+b)°$

$= \cos a° \cos b° - \sin a° \sin b°$ ✓

$= \frac{3}{5} \times \frac{5}{13} - \frac{4}{5} \times \frac{12}{13}$ ✓ ✓

$= \frac{15}{65} - \frac{48}{65} = -\frac{33}{65}$ ✓

4 marks

Expansion
- You are given the formula:

  cos (A ± B) = cos A cos B ∓ sin A sin B during your exam.

Angle *a*° ratios
- $\sin a° = \frac{4}{5}$ and $\cos a° = \frac{3}{5}$.

Angle *b*° ratios
- $\sin b° = \frac{12}{13}$ and $\cos b° = \frac{5}{13}$.

Calculation
- This mark is for the correct substitution and subsequent calculation.

HMRN: p. 35

Q1(*b*)

$\sin(a+b)°$

$= \sin a° \cos b° + \cos a° \sin b°$ ✓

$= \frac{4}{5} \times \frac{5}{13} + \frac{3}{5} \times \frac{12}{13}$

$= \frac{20}{65} + \frac{36}{65} = \frac{56}{65}$ ✓

2 marks

Expansion
- You are given the formula:

  sin (A ± B) = sin A cos B ± cos A sin B during your exam.

Calculation
- You are using these rules for fractions:

  $\frac{a}{b} \times \frac{c}{d} = \frac{ac}{bd}$ and $\frac{a}{c} + \frac{b}{c} = \frac{a+b}{c}$.

Q1(*c*)

$$\tan(a+b)° = \frac{\sin(a+b)°}{\cos(a+b)°}$$

$$= \frac{\frac{56}{65}}{\frac{-33}{65}} = \frac{\frac{56}{65} \times 65}{\frac{-33}{65} \times 65}$$

$$= -\frac{56}{33}$$ ✓

1 mark

Formula & calculation
- You are using the result $\tan x° = \frac{\sin x°}{\cos x°}$ and then substituting the exact values that you calculated in parts (*a*) and (*b*).
- An alternative simplification process is:

  $\frac{56}{65} \div \left(-\frac{33}{65}\right) = -\frac{56}{65} \times \frac{65}{33} = -\frac{56}{33}$ (after cancelling the two 65 factors).
- Note that in all parts of this question you are wrong to use decimals since all the questions state "exact value". You would lose marks for "going decimal".

HMRN: p. 36

Q2

$$\int \frac{2-x^5}{x^3}\,dx$$

$$=\int \frac{2}{x^3}-\frac{x^5}{x^3}\,dx$$

$$=\int 2x^{-3}-x^2\,dx \quad ✓$$

$$=\frac{2x^{-2}}{-2}-\frac{x^3}{3}+C \quad ✓ ✓$$

$$=-\frac{1}{x^2}-\frac{x^3}{3}+C \quad ✓$$

4 marks

Integrable form

- You have to prepare $\frac{2-x^5}{x^3}$ for integration by 1st "splitting the fraction": $\frac{2}{x^3}-\frac{x^5}{x^3}$ and then changing each term to the form ax^n.

1st integration

- This mark is for $\frac{2x^{-2}}{-2}$.

2nd integration

- This mark is for $-\frac{x^3}{3}$.

Result

- Remember to include C, the constant of integration.

HMRN: p. 31

Q3(*a*)

$$\overrightarrow{CA}=\boldsymbol{a}-\boldsymbol{c}=\begin{pmatrix}3\\2\\5\end{pmatrix}-\begin{pmatrix}6\\4\\3\end{pmatrix}=\begin{pmatrix}-3\\-2\\2\end{pmatrix} \quad ✓$$

$$\overrightarrow{CB}=\boldsymbol{b}-\boldsymbol{c}=\begin{pmatrix}6\\0\\3\end{pmatrix}-\begin{pmatrix}6\\4\\3\end{pmatrix}=\begin{pmatrix}0\\-4\\0\end{pmatrix} \quad ✓$$

2 marks

Components

- You are using the basic position vector result: $\overrightarrow{PQ}=\boldsymbol{q}-\boldsymbol{p}$

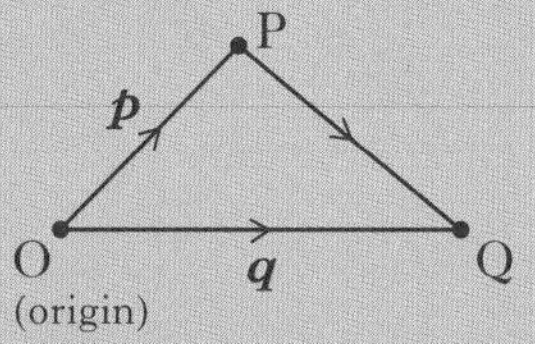

If you travel from P to Q (in the diagram above) via the origin you encounter $-\boldsymbol{p}$ (against the arrow) then $\boldsymbol{q}$, i.e $-\boldsymbol{p}+\boldsymbol{q}$ which is the same as $\boldsymbol{q}-\boldsymbol{p}$ $(\boldsymbol{q}+(-\boldsymbol{p}))$.

Components

- Take care over the order: $\boldsymbol{b}-\boldsymbol{c}$, not $\boldsymbol{c}-\boldsymbol{b}$.

HMRN: p. 42

Q3(*b*)

Use $\cos\theta^\circ = \dfrac{\boldsymbol{p}\cdot\boldsymbol{q}}{|\boldsymbol{p}||\boldsymbol{q}|}$

with $\boldsymbol{p} = \begin{pmatrix}-3\\-2\\2\end{pmatrix}$ and $\boldsymbol{q} = \begin{pmatrix}0\\-4\\0\end{pmatrix}$ ✓

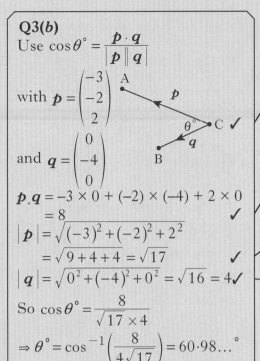

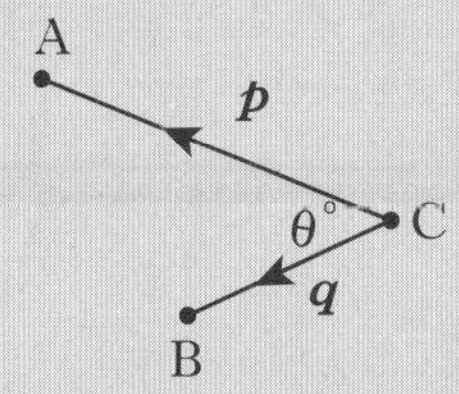

$\boldsymbol{p}.\boldsymbol{q} = -3 \times 0 + (-2) \times (-4) + 2 \times 0$

$= 8$ ✓

$|\boldsymbol{p}| = \sqrt{(-3)^2 + (-2)^2 + 2^2}$

$= \sqrt{9+4+4} = \sqrt{17}$ ✓

$|\boldsymbol{q}| = \sqrt{0^2 + (-4)^2 + 0^2} = \sqrt{16} = 4$ ✓

So $\cos\theta^\circ = \dfrac{8}{\sqrt{17} \times 4}$

$\Rightarrow \theta^\circ = \cos^{-1}\left(\dfrac{8}{4\sqrt{17}}\right) = 60{\cdot}98\ldots^\circ$

The angle between edges CA and CB is approximately 61·0° ✓ (to 1 decimal place).

5 marks

Strategy

- You should know to use the scalar product to find the angle between two vectors.

Scalar product

- $\begin{pmatrix}x_1\\y_1\\z_1\end{pmatrix}\cdot\begin{pmatrix}x_2\\y_2\\z_2\end{pmatrix} = x_1x_2 + y_1y_2 + z_1z_2$. The corresponding components are multiplied and the results added.

Magnitude

- The result used is $\left|\begin{pmatrix}a\\b\\c\end{pmatrix}\right| = \sqrt{a^2+b^2+c^2}$.

Magnitude

- Remember in these calculations that squaring negative quantities results in a positive answer.

Angle

- Be careful with the keying sequence on your calculator. Either calculate $8 \div (4 \times \sqrt{17})$ and then $\cos^{-1}$(ANS) or use the sequence:
  [cos⁻¹][(][8][÷][(][4][×][√][1][7][)][)]
- Degrees or radians are acceptable: 1·06 radians (to 3 significant figures).

HMRN: p. 46

Q4(*a*)

O(0, 0) and P(6, 2)

Midpoint of $\text{OP} = \text{M}\left(\dfrac{0+6}{2}, \dfrac{0+2}{2}\right)$

$= \text{M}(3, 1)$ ✓

$m_{\text{OP}} = \dfrac{2}{6} = \dfrac{1}{3} \Rightarrow m_\perp = -3$ ✓

For the perpendicular bisector: gradient = –3, a point on the line is (3, 1).

The equation is $y - 1 = -3(x - 3)$

$\Rightarrow y - 1 = -3x + 9$

$\Rightarrow y = -3x + 10$ ✓

$\Rightarrow y + 3x = 10$

3 marks

Midpoint

- The midpoint M of the line joining $\text{A}(x_1, y_1)$ to $\text{B}(x_2, y_2)$ is given by: $\text{M}\left(\dfrac{x_1+x_2}{2}, \dfrac{y_1+y_2}{2}\right)$.

Perpendicular gradient

- If $m = \dfrac{a}{b}$ then $m_\perp = -\dfrac{b}{a}$

so $m = \dfrac{1}{3}$ gives $m_\perp = -\dfrac{3}{1} = -3$.

Equation

- The line passing through (a, b) with gradient m is $y - b = m(x - a)$. In this case $a = 3$, $b = 1$ and $m = -3$.

HMRN: p. 4–6

Q4(*b*)

$y - 2x + 10 = 0$

$\Rightarrow y = 2x - 10$ ✓

$\Rightarrow m_{\text{tangent}} = 2$ ✓

$\Rightarrow m_{\perp} = -\frac{1}{2}$

$\Rightarrow m_{PQ} = -\frac{1}{2}$ ✓

For the radius QP:

The gradient $= -\frac{1}{2}$

a point on the line is (6, 2)

So the equation is

$y - 2 = -\frac{1}{2}(x - 6)$

$\Rightarrow 2y - 4 = -x + 6$

$\Rightarrow 2y + x = 10$ ✓

4 marks

Rearrangement
- This strategy mark is for knowing to compare the given equation with the standard form $y = mx + c$ to determine the gradient m.

Gradient of tangent
- In this case comparing $y = mx + c$ leads to the value $m = 2$ for the tangent.
- Try to check your answers with the given diagram to see if they are reasonable: $m = 2$ implies "1 along, 2 up" which matches the tangent shown in the diagram.

Gradient of radius
- The tangent is perpendicular to the radius from the centre of the circle to the point of contact P.
- You are using the perpendicular gradient result: $m = \frac{a}{b} \Rightarrow m_{\perp} = -\frac{b}{a}$. In this case:
  $m = 2 = \frac{2}{1} \Rightarrow m_{\perp} = -\frac{1}{2}$

Equation
- You are using $y - b = m(x - a)$ with (a, b) being (6, 2) and $m = -\frac{1}{2}$.
- It is usual to clear the fractions from the resulting equation. In this case you are multiplying both sides of the equation by 2.

HMRN: p. 4–6

Q4(*c*)

Point Q is the intersection of MQ and PQ so solve:

$$\left.\begin{aligned} y + 3x &= 10 \\ 2y + x &= 10 \end{aligned}\right\} \overset{\times 2}{\Rightarrow} \begin{aligned} 2y + 6x &= 20 \\ 2y + x &= 10 \end{aligned}$$ ✓

Subtract: $5x = 10$

$\Rightarrow x = 2$ ✓

Now substitute $x = 2$ in the equation $y + 3x = 10$

$\Rightarrow y + 6 = 10 \Rightarrow y = 4$

So Q(2, 4) ✓

3 marks

Strategy
- As in many questions in Paper 2, the answers to previous parts of the question are used in subsequent parts.
- You should know the centre of a circle will lie on the perpendicular bisector of a chord of the circle (in this case chord OP). So from parts (*a*) and (*b*), you have the equations of two lines that the centre lies on, and the centre therefore lies at their intersection point. You are using simultaneous equations to find this point of intersection.

1st coordinate
- Alternatively, by multiplying equation 2 by 3:

$$\left.\begin{aligned} y + 3x &= 10 \\ 6y + 3x &= 30 \end{aligned}\right\}$$ subtraction leads to $5y = 20 \Rightarrow y = 4$

2nd coordinate
- Either equation will do for this substitution.

HMRN: p. 6

Q5

$$f(x) = \frac{2}{3\sqrt{x}} = \frac{2}{3x^{\frac{1}{2}}} = \frac{2}{3}x^{-\frac{1}{2}}$$ ✓

$$\Rightarrow f'(x) = -\frac{1}{2} \times \frac{2}{3}x^{-\frac{3}{2}} = -\frac{1}{3}x^{-\frac{3}{2}}$$ ✓

$$= -\frac{1}{3x^{\frac{3}{2}}} = -\frac{1}{3\left(\sqrt{x}\right)^3}$$ ✓

So $f'(1) = -\frac{1}{3\left(\sqrt{1}\right)^3} = -\frac{1}{3}$ ✓

also $f(1) = \frac{2}{3\sqrt{1}} = \frac{2}{3}$ ✓

For the tangent:

gradient $= -\frac{1}{3}$

a point on the line is $\left(1, \frac{2}{3}\right)$

So the equation is:

$$y - \frac{2}{3} = -\frac{1}{3}(x-1)$$
$$\Rightarrow 3y - 2 = -(x-1)$$
$$\Rightarrow 3y - 2 = -x + 1$$
$$\Rightarrow 3y = -x + 3$$ ✓

6 marks

Strategy

- You should know that to find the equation of the tangent you first need to differentiate. This is essential to find the gradient of the tangent.

Preparation for differentiating

- To use the differentiation rules that you have learnt, the expression $\frac{2}{3\sqrt{x}}$ needs to be prepared for differentiating. This involves changing the expression to the form ax^n so that the following rule can be used:

$$f(x) = ax^n \Rightarrow f'(x) = anx^{n-1}$$

- $\sqrt{x}$ is written $x^{1/2}$
- When $x^{\frac{1}{2}}$ appears as a factor on the bottom of the fraction it can be moved "up" to appear as the factor $x^{-\frac{1}{2}}$ on the top of the fraction. To do this you are using the rule:

$$x^{-n} = \frac{1}{x^n}$$

- Notice that $\frac{2x^{-\frac{1}{2}}}{3}$ and $\frac{2}{3}x^{-\frac{1}{2}}$ are the same.

A simpler example is $\frac{x}{2} = \frac{1}{2}x$.

Differentiate

- This mark is for $-\frac{1}{3}x^{-\frac{3}{2}}$

Evaluate

- Although it is possible, using your calculator, to evaluate $f'(1)$ in the form $-\frac{1}{3}x^{-\frac{3}{2}}$, you should know how to "prepare for evaluating" by changing to the form $-\frac{1}{3\left(\sqrt{x}\right)^3}$. This is important for Paper 1 questions where you have no calculator available.

***y*-coordinate**

- $f'(1)$ gives the gradient when $x = 1$ and $f(1)$ gives the y-coordinate of the point of contact of the tangent on the curve.

Equation

- You are using $y - b = m(x - a)$ where $a = 1$, $b = \frac{2}{3}$ and $m = -\frac{1}{3}$.

HMRN: p. 19–20

Q6

To find the points of intersection of the graphs: ✓

Solve:

$$\left.\begin{aligned} y &= x+1 \\ y &= x^2-1 \end{aligned}\right\} \begin{aligned} &\Rightarrow x^2-1 = x+1 \\ &\Rightarrow x^2-x-2=0 \end{aligned}$$

$$\Rightarrow (x-2)(x+1)=0$$

$$\Rightarrow x=2 \text{ or } x=-1 \quad ✓$$

The shaded area is given by: ✓

$$\int_{-1}^{2}(x+1)-(x^2-1)\,dx \quad ✓$$

$$=\int_{-1}^{2} x+1-x^2+1\;dx$$

$$=\int_{-1}^{2} x-x^2+2\;dx \quad ✓$$

$$=\left[\frac{x^2}{2}-\frac{x^3}{3}+2x\right]_{-1}^{2} \quad ✓$$

$$=\left(\frac{2^2}{2}-\frac{2^3}{3}+2\times 2\right)-\left(\frac{(-1)^2}{2}-\frac{(-1)^3}{3}+2\times(-1)\right) \quad ✓$$

$$=2-\frac{8}{3}+4-\left(\frac{1}{2}+\frac{1}{3}-2\right)$$

$$=2-\frac{8}{3}+4-\frac{1}{2}-\frac{1}{3}+2$$

$$=\frac{12}{6}-\frac{16}{6}+\frac{24}{6}-\frac{3}{6}-\frac{2}{6}+\frac{12}{6}$$

$$=\frac{27}{6}=\frac{9}{2}\text{ unit}^2 \quad ✓$$

8 marks

Strategy
- You will need to find the points of intersection of the two graphs to get the limits for the integral.

Solve equation
- Set the two equations equal to obtain a quadratic equation.
- You should always check that your solutions (in this case $x = 2$ and $x = -1$) match the graph diagram given in the question ($x = 2$ corresponds to point Q, $x = -1$ corresponds to point P).

Strategy
- You are using $\int \left(\begin{smallmatrix}\text{top}\\ \text{curve}\end{smallmatrix}\right)-\left(\begin{smallmatrix}\text{bottom}\\ \text{curve}\end{smallmatrix}\right) dx$ for the area.

Limits
- The area you are finding stretches from $x = -1$ to $x = 2$ (left to right) so the limits on the integral sign are -1 and 2 (bottom to top).

Integral
- The 'top' curve minus the 'bottom' curve gives $(x + 1) - (x^2 - 1)$ and this subtraction must be in the correct order.
- Note that the brackets around $x^2 - 1$ are essential, giving $-x^2 + 1$ when they are removed.
- This mark is for obtaining $x - x^2 + 2$.

Integration
- You are using: $\int x^n\,dx = \frac{x^{n+1}}{n+1} + C$ and $\int a\,dx = ax + C$ for the integration. The C is not needed when there are limits on the integral sign.

Substitute limits
- 1st substitute the "top" limit ($x = 2$) then substitute the "bottom" limit ($x = -1$) and subtract.

Calculation
- Mistakes can easily be made in a complicated calculation like this. Always double-check your work.

HMRN: p. 33

Q7(*a*)

For Jan 1 2000 set $t = 0$

$$p = 6\times e^{0\cdot0138\times 0}$$

$$= 6\times e^{0} = 6\times 1 = 6 \quad ✓$$

The population was 6 billion.

1 mark

Evaluation
- The crucial phrase is "t years after January 1, 2000". With $t = 0$ you get "0 years after January 1, 2000" in other words: January 1, 2000!
- The index law $a^0 = 1$ for any value of a (other than 0) is used here.

Q7(*b*)

Solve: $12 = 6\,e^{0\cdot0138t}$ ✓

$\Rightarrow 2 = e^{0\cdot0138t}$

$\Rightarrow \log_e 2 = 0\cdot0138t$ ✓

$\Rightarrow t = \dfrac{\log_e 2}{0\cdot0138} = 50\cdot22\ldots$ ✓

So during 2050 the population reaches 12 billion.
At the start of 2051 the population will be more than double its level in 2000. ✓

4 marks

Equation
- Having established in part (*a*) that 6 billion was the population on January 1, 2000 the question is asking for the value of *t* that will give a population of 12 billion (double 6 billion), i.e. set P = 12 in the formula.

Logarithmic form
- You are using $a = b^c \Leftrightarrow \log_b a = c$

Calculation
- The key ln calculates log to the base *e*.

Interpretation
- You need to take care over the wording of the question: "at the start of which year". So 2050 is not correct. At the start of 2050 the population had not yet reached 12 billion.

HMRN: p. 51

Q8(*a*)

$a = -1,\ b = 2$ ✓

1 mark

Values
- Notice that $y = f(x)$ is the sine curve reflected in the *x*-axis. The *y*-coordinates of points on the sine curve have changed sign.
- For $y = g(x)$: this is a cosine curve with two cycles from 0 to 2π giving $b = 2$.

HMRN: p. 16

Q8(*b*)

$f(x) = -\sin x$ and $g(x) = \cos 2x$

$f(x) = g(x) \Rightarrow -\sin x = \cos 2x$

$\Rightarrow -\sin x = 1 - 2\sin^2 x$ ✓

$\Rightarrow 2\sin^2 x - \sin x - 1 = 0$

$\Rightarrow (2\sin x + 1)(\sin x - 1) = 0$ ✓

$\Rightarrow 2\sin x + 1 = 0$ or $\sin x - 1 = 0$

$\Rightarrow \sin x = -\frac{1}{2}$ or $\sin x = 1$ ✓

For $\sin x = -\frac{1}{2}$, the negative value indicates that *x* is in the 3rd or 4th quadrants. This corresponds to points B and C. $\sin x = 1$ $\left(x = \frac{\pi}{2}\right)$ corresponds to point A as required. ✓

4 marks

Strategy
- There are three possibilities for $\cos 2x$: $2\cos^2 x - 1$, $\cos^2 x - \sin^2 x$ and $1 - 2\sin^2 x$. This last version has only '$\sin x$' and this matches the left-hand side of the equation.

Factorisation
- Compare $2a^2 - a - 1 = 0$ giving $(2a + 1)(a - 1) = 0$.

Solutions
- There are two possible values for $\sin x$ at this stage.

Interpretation
- You need to eliminate the possibility that $\sin x = -\frac{1}{2}$. At this stage you should refer to the diagram for the question to try to interpret your solutions and identify the points on the graph that correspond to each of your two solutions.

HMRN: p. 37

Q9(*a*)

-2	1	$2-a$	$-a$	$2a$
		-2	$2a$	$-2a$
	1	$-a$	a	0

so $f(-2) = 0$ ✓

1 mark

Calculation

- An alternative is to substitute $x = -2$ in $x^3 + (2 - a)x^2 - ax + 2a$, giving

$(-2)^3 + (2 - a)(-2)^2 - a(-2) + 2a$

$= -8 + 4(2 - a) + 2a + 2a$

$= -8 + 8 - 4a + 2a + 2a$

$= 0$ and so $f(-2) = 0$

HMRN: p. 25

Q9(*b*)

From part (*a*) above: ✓

$f(x) = (x+2)(x^2 - ax + a)$ ✓

$f(x) = 0 \Rightarrow (x+2)(x^2 - ax + a) = 0$

$\Rightarrow x + 2 = 0$ or $x^2 - ax + a = 0$

If only one root is required it will be $x = -2$ and so $x^2 - ax + a = 0$ will have no Real roots. ✓

Discriminant

$= (-a)^2 - 4 \times 1 \times a$ ✓

$= a^2 - 4a = a(a-4)$ ✓

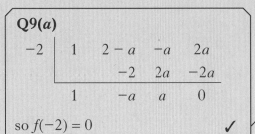

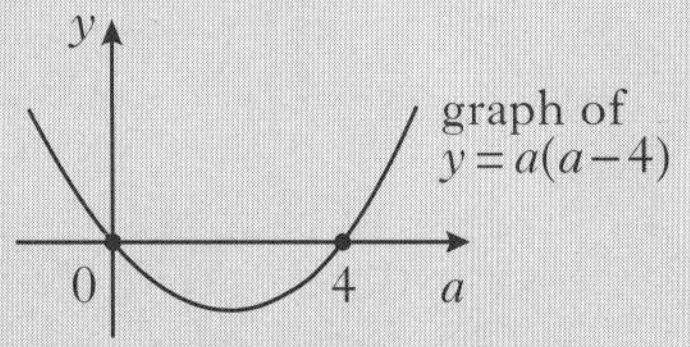

✓

You require Discriminant < 0

$\Rightarrow$ $0 < a < 4$ which is the required range of values ✓

7 marks

Strategy

- This mark is for the use of synthetic division (which in the given solution was used in part (*a*)).
- Synthetic division is necessary so that the cubic expression can be factorised.

Quadratic factor

- In the bottom row of the synthetic division table the terms: $1, -a, a$ appear. Since you started with a cubic (degree 3) you will end up with a quadratic (degree 2) and these terms are the coefficients of this quadratic factor, i.e. $1x^2 - ax + a$.

Strategy

- You will be examining the discriminant for the quadratic equation $x^2 - ax + a = 0$ to impose a "no Real roots" condition.

Discriminant

- '$b^2 - 4a'c$' with $b = -a$, $a' = 1$ and $c = a$ (note that there are two distinct letter *a*'s used here – confusing!)

Factorisation

- This mark is for $a(a - 4)$ appearing.

Strategy

- How do you solve $a^2 - 4a < 0$? The solution graphs the values of $a^2 - 4a$ and you can then pick out values of a where the graph lies below the "a-axis".

Range

- Note that $a > 0$ <u>and</u> $a < 4$: both conditions are necessary. $0 < a < 4$ is the best way of describing these conditions. "$a > 0$ or $a < 4$" is not correct as this allows the possibility that only one condition is true.

HMRN: p. 26–29